THE FIRST LADY IS NEWS!

No one who watched the January 26, 1992, episode of *60 Minutes* will ever forget the face of Hillary Clinton, when she appeared at her husband's side and laid bare the roots of their marriage. Intense blue eyes flashing, her lips held crisply in a smile that occasionally cracked with suppressed anger, she turned her piercing gaze at the nation's viewers and said: Here we are. Take us or leave us. If you don't like what we say, don't vote for us.

Out of that nightmarish moment, a phenomenon was born. Hillary Rodham Clinton burned her way into the American psyche. Little did she know that she would be chosen along with Bill Clinton's draft record, and even his alleged infidelities, as a choice target of attack in the volatile 1992 campaign. At the other extreme, who could have guessed that this blue-eyed, blonde, very successful lawyer would become a rallying point for a generation of young professional women and working mothers?

This fascinating, dazzle-and-warts-and-all biography reveals the complex, often contradictory woman behind the headlines. It offers a candid look at our new First Lady—who she is, where she's been, and what her new role will mean for the American public.

JUDITH WARNER began her career in journalism in the prestigious Writing Program at the *New York Times*, for which she wrote frequently for the Science, Living, and Education sections. She is currently on leave from *Ms.* magazine, where she recently edited the *Ms.* election guide. Her articles have appeared in numerous publications, including *New York Woman*, *McCall's*, *New York Observer*, and the *Boston Globe*. She lives in New York City.

Ⓜ MENTOR   (0451)

READINGS IN U.S. HISTORY

☐ **A DOCUMENTARY HISTORY OF THE UNITED STATES by Richard D. Heffner.** A unique collection—57 important documents that have shaped America's history, with a commentary showing their significance.

(624130—$6.99)

☐ **THE FEDERALIST PAPERS edited and with an Introduction by Clinton Rossiter.** Written by Alexander Hamilton, James Madison, and John Jay, the Federalist Papers defended the concept of a strong central government with their arguments in favor of the Constitution. Scholars have long regarded this work as a milestone in political science and a classic of American political theory.   (625412—$5.95)

☐ **THE ANTI-FEDERALIST PAPERS edited and with an Introduction by Ralph Kecham.** Revealing the dissenting opinions of such statesmen as Patrick Henry and John DeWitt, who saw in the Federalist Papers as threats to rights and liberties so recently won from England. The Anti-Federalist Papers represent an important contribution to the American political tradition.   (625250—$4.99)

☐ **THE LIVING U.S. CONSTITUTION by Saul K. Padover.** A comprehensive, expanded, and completely updated guide to understanding the Constitution and the men who framed it. Includes the complete text of the Constitution with an informative index, historic Supreme Court decisions, and new precedent-setting cases concerning civil liberties. Second Revised Edition.

(621743—$4.95)

Prices slightly higher in Canada

Buy them at your local bookstore or use this convenient coupon for ordering.

NEW AMERICAN LIBRARY
P.O. Box 999 – Dept. #17109
Bergenfield, New Jersey 07621

Please send me the books I have checked above.
I am enclosing $_____ (please add $2.00 to cover postage and handling).
Send check or money order (no cash or C.O.D.'s) or charge by Mastercard or VISA (with a $15.00 minimum). Prices and numbers are subject to change without notice.

Card #_____ Exp. Date _____
Signature_____
Name_____
Address_____
City _____ State _____ Zip Code _____

For faster service when ordering by credit card call **1-800-253-6476**
Allow a minimum of 4-6 weeks for delivery. This offer is subject to change without notice.

HILLARY CLINTON

THE INSIDE STORY

JUDITH WARNER

A SIGNET BOOK

SIGNET
Published by the Penguin Group
Penguin Books USA Inc., 375 Hudson Street,
New York, New York 10014, U.S.A.
Penguin Books Ltd, 27 Wrights Lane,
London W8 5TZ, England
Penguin Books Australia Ltd, Ringwood,
Victoria, Australia
Penguin Books Canada Ltd, 10 Alcorn Avenue,
Toronto, Ontario, Canada M4V 3B2
Penguin Books (N.Z.) Ltd, 182–190 Wairau Road,
Auckland 10, New Zealand

Penguin Books Ltd, Registered Offices:
Harmondsworth, Middlesex, England

First published by Signet, an imprint of New American Library, a
division of Penguin Books USA Inc.

First Printing, January, 1993
10 9 8 7 6 5 4 3 2 1

Copyright © Judith Warner, 1993
All rights reserved

Cover photo: Cynthia Johnson/*Time* magazine

 REGISTERED TRADEMARK—MARCA REGISTRADA

Printed in the United States of America

Without limiting the rights under copyright reserved above, no part of
this publication may be reproduced, stored in or introduced into a
retrieval system, or transmitted, in any form, or by any means (elec-
tronic, mechanical, photocopying, recording, or otherwise), without
the prior written permission of both the copyright owner and the
above publisher of this book.

BOOKS ARE AVAILABLE AT QUANTITY DISCOUNTS WHEN
USED TO PROMOTE PRODUCTS OR SERVICES. FOR INFOR-
MATION PLEASE WRITE TO PREMIUM MARKETING DIVI-
SION, PENGUIN BOOKS USA INC., 375 HUDSON STREET,
NEW YORK, NEW YORK 10014.

If you purchased this book without a cover you should be aware that
this book is stolen property. It was reported as "unsold and de-
stroyed" to the publisher and neither the author nor the publisher has
received any payment for this "stripped book."

Contents

Acknowledgments

The writing of this book would not have been possible without Max Berley, who conducted many of the interviews and did much of the reporting.

I would also like to thank Lisa Caputo, the Reverend Don Jones, Gloria Steinem, Naomi Wolf, Ruth Mandel, Fred Altshuler, Brownie Ledbetter, Thomas F. (Mack) McLarty, Betsey Wright, Connie Fails, Carolyn Staley, Richard Stearns, Eleanor Acheson, Nancy Snyderman, Professor Alan Schechter, Morton and Patricia Fry, Allan Bersin, Bill Coleman, Phyllis Brandon, Max and Ellen Brantley, and Eleanor McGovern for their generous contributions of time and reflection, as well as the numerous people I interviewed who asked to remain unidentified.

I am particularly indebted to Charles Flynn Allen, who permitted me the free use of interview transcripts used in preparation for this book *The Comeback Kid*, co-written with Jonathan Portis. Articles and interviews by Garry Wills, Christopher Buchard, Eleanor Clift, and Gail Sheehy provided invaluable background material. I want to thank the *Arkansas Democrat-Gazette* for the use of their library, Liza Featherstone for her substantive research, and the staff of *Ms.* magazine for their support and encouragement throughout this project. Kimberly Witherspoon deserves a special thanks for making it all happen. And thanks, too, to Porter Bibb, without whose encouragement this book never would have been written.

Do all the good you can, in all the ways you can, in all the places you can, at all the times you can, to all the people you can, as long as ever you can.

—JOHN WESLEY

Introduction

The Most Powerful Woman in the World

In late January 1991, Hillary Rodham Clinton took Chelsea Clinton to San Francisco to spend a holiday weekend with three of her closest friends and their daughters.

The mother-daughter weekend had been planned long in advance. It meant rearranging schedules, co-ordinating vacations, and braving the skies at a time when the Gulf War was raging and reports of possible terrorist attacks on the nation's airports were on the rise.

Hillary Clinton wouldn't have missed the trip for anything. For four glorious days she, her friends, and their rambunctious young daughters rowed boats in Sausalito, ate Chinese take-out food, visited the city's planetarium, and generally talked up a storm.

There was only one ripple during their blissful days. One afternoon, while the friends sat contentedly drinking Irish coffee in a curbside San Francisco café, a passerby stopped and asked one of them if she might by any chance be the famous actress Mary Steenburgen.

Yes, Steenburgen said with a grimace, I am.

The passerby then rounded the table and asked Steenburgen's neighbor if she was the television reporter and talk-show host Nancy Snyderman.

Yes, Snyderman said. Yes, indeed.

Once the passerby passed out of sight, Hillary Clinton, first lady of Arkansas, turned to face Little Rock dress designer Connie Fails, and smiled. "Isn't it great," she said, "to be out of Arkansas where nobody knows who we are?"

So much can happen in two years.

Hillary Clinton will never again be able to walk down a city street unrecognized. She won't be doing much sitting in cafés now either. It's good-bye to driving her Buick around town. So long to family nights at the movies—saving seats in the center with Chelsea while Bill saunters up to the concession stand to buy popcorn. No more impromptu workouts at the YWCA. No more taking Chelsea shopping, Secret Service-free, at the mall. No more quiet corner office at the Rose Law Firm in Little Rock. They'd hung a banner outside her office window election night: "We're Proud of You, Hillary."

Good-bye to all that.

Her name is now a household word.

"Hillary! Hillary!"

The crowd standing outside on the Old State House lawn shouted her name during Bill Clinton's acceptance speech. Momentarily, they drowned him out, on the very night he was elected the forty-second president of the United States.

He had to grin, just a bit.

"You can cheer for her," he said.

"Hillary! Hillary! Hillary!" they roared.

Hillary Clinton is perhaps the first first lady with whom 280 million Americans feel they are on a first-name basis.

She is "Hillary," the evil witch, a slur off the tongue of Pat Buchanan at the Republican National Convention; Hillary the heroine of young women and working mothers; Hillary the former co-candidate, smiling from buttons that urged "VOTE FOR HILLARY'S HUSBAND." On newsstands in Europe this November, she made front-page headlines after the election. "HILLARY'S HUSBAND ELECTED," Berlin's *Tageszeitung* announced. France's *Paris-Match* said she was "The Woman Who Built His Victory." *BZ*, another Berlin daily, simply called her: "THE MOST POWERFUL WOMAN IN THE WORLD."

A week before the election, Hillary Clinton, riding in the back of a limousine to an airport and chatting with *New York Times* columnist Anna Quindlen, admitted that her fame was growing faster than she could keep up with it. How did she feel, she was asked, about becoming the most powerful woman in the world, a role model to millions.

She was somewhat at a loss to answer. "That feeling has been sweeping over me," she answered feebly. "I feel the responsibility so much."

"We're just going to roll the dice and see what happens."

It was only a year ago that Hillary Clinton made her mark upon the minds of America's news watchers, with her ground-breaking appearance on the January 26, 1992 episode of *60 Minutes*. No one who watched that special show will ever forget the face of the future first lady as she appeared at her husband's side and laid bare the roots of their marriage. Intense blue eyes flashing, lips held crisply in a smile that occasionally cracked with suppressed anger, she turned to the nation's viewers with a piercing gaze that said, *What you see is what you get. Take us or leave us.* "And, you know, if that's not enough for people, then, heck, don't vote for him."

Out of this nightmarish moment a phenomenon was born. Hillary Rodham Clinton—lawyer, activist, mother, political wife, feminist—burned her way into the American psyche. Little did she know that she would be chosen over Bill Clinton's draft record, and even a flowery lounge singer named Gennifer, as the Republican party's Willie Horton of the 1992 campaign. Little did this churchgoing former Goldwater Girl suspect that, in a few months' time, she'd be cast as a modern-day Lilith by the likes of Pat Robertson, Pat Buchanan, and Marilyn Quayle. At the other extreme, who would have guessed that this blue-eyed, blond-haired, headband-wearing lawyer wife of the Democratic candidate for president would become a rallying point for a generation of young, professional women and working mothers?

"I sometimes wonder how history gets written," Hillary Clinton once said, with the tinge of wariness so typical of her public style. While she was on the campaign trail last year, she often expressed puzzlement that her life and words received as much press attention as world events.

"It's so hard," she told *Glamour* last April, "to keep people's attention focused on what will matter in their own lives."

As the lesson of the last year's campaign has shown, Hillary Clinton *is* what matters in people's lives. As a symbol of all that is good or bad about American women today, her name has become the most hotly traded currency in America's culture wars since the Equal Rights Amendment. By being who she is, and embodying what she stands for, Hillary Rodham Clinton has become a figure in American social history. She is the first candidate's wife who, by a combination of personality, timing, and circumstance, has succeeded in dividing the nation. Her life mirrors those of women who came of age in the social upheavals of the late 1960s, married and/or built careers in the 1970s, reached professional stature in the 1980s, and by the election year of 1992 had come to symbolize, for the right, all that was wrong with American life, and for the left, both evolution and compromise.

Hillary Clinton graduated from college in 1969, just as the American women's movement was picking up steam. Like many other women of her turbulent generation, she struggled throughout her early adult life with the dilemmas of career versus marriage, tradition versus innovation, loyalty versus pride. She left law school with dreams of glory in Washington. She then "followed her heart" to Arkansas to build a life helping the man she loved achieve elected office. She gave up full-time legal activism to make a name for herself as a corporate lawyer—and to support her family. She ended up earning four times her husband's salary. Though she quickly made partner in her firm, was instrumental in overhauling Arkansas's substandard educational system, and was twice named one of America's hundred best lawyers, she did not fulfill her activist dream.

Hillary Clinton's life represents both the triumphs and the sacrifices of women of her generation. In 1978, when Bill Clinton was first elected governor of Arkansas, Hillary was considered somewhat of a handicap. Her look had changed little since her left-leaning college days. She wore no makeup, hid behind thick glasses, dressed in big, shapeless sweaters and sacklike skirts, and did little to tame the mousy, meandering waves of her hair. She shocked Clinton's constituents by keeping her maiden name—even when their daughter, Chelsea, was born. She was a contributing factor in his reelection defeat in 1980.

When Clinton sprung back in the 1982 election, however, he had a new-looking wife by his side. She had dyed her hair, traded in her glasses for contact lenses, and bought a new wardrobe. She had even taken his name. At Clinton's inauguration that year, she wore a beaded gown of silk and lace, and the fashion brigades gushed approval. She started wearing hats on Easter Sunday. She passed.

The lessons of that year served her well. When Bill Clinton's presidential campaign made new demands of her image a decade later, she knew how to react. She knew what was important and what was not. She got rid of the headband. And when that wasn't enough, her public personality went into remission. From the tough, outspoken lawyer, the co-candidate with strong feminist ties, she became a strong but dutiful wife, proudly standing by her man across a podium from Tipper Gore and hers. When her loyal speeches and strategizing began to be seen as too abrasive, she toned herself down, tried pastels, and by the time of the Democratic National Convention kept in tune with the festivities by pushing her recipe for chocolate chip cookies. When it was safe to come out again, after the Republican convention, she was back on the trail in full force, pounding her pulpits, striking hard. When her husband lost his voice temporarily, she spoke for him. On election night, she handed him the note cards for his acceptance speech. Their partnership has withstood the test of time and public bashing. But it did not do so without a personal cost to Hillary.

This past year she faced belittlement in the press, partisan barbs about her integrity, outright hatred directed at her, the candidate's *wife*, by the Republicans at the convention. It was fortunate that she had already developed a thick skin in Arkansas. "What I represent is generational change," she told the public on the *Today* show. "It's not about me."

That is true. Hillary Clinton, in the last election year, became a sort of mirror reflecting America's anxieties about the evolution of gender relations, two-salary households, and marriage itself. Just as the country has wavered wildly in accepting the social changes of the past twenty-five years, it maintained an ambivalent relationship with Hillary Clinton, sometimes loving her, sometimes hating her, almost always, to some degree, fearing her. The public's fascination with Hillary was a fascination with itself. When she was hated, and when she was loved, American society was racked by what it loves and hates in itself.

Hillary Rodham Clinton has been made into an icon for our age. And now, as she embarks on her first term in the White House, it is time she becomes known as a real person, too.

Hillary Diane was born in Chicago on October 26, 1947, to parents Dorothy and Hugh Rodham. Her father owned a small textile business. She grew up a Methodist and was strongly influenced by a youth minister who took the church's teenagers on visits to poor black and Hispanic neighborhoods in downtown Chicago.

In 1965, she traveled east to Wellesley College, where, at her graduation in 1969, she delivered their first student commencement speech ever. She used her time in part to upbraid her fellow speaker, Senator Edward Brooke, for his lack of "relevance." As a result of her impertinence, her picture appeared in *Life* magazine.

After Wellesley, she went on to Yale Law School, where she demonstrated against discrimination, helped edit an alternative law journal, and met Bill Clinton. She spent a year doing a special study of child development and family law, and after graduation, put her interests to work as a lawyer for the Children's Defense Fund. She spent six months working as legal counsel on the special impeachment staff of the House Judiciary Committee that was investigating charges against President Richard Nixon. She moved to Fayetteville, Arkansas, in 1974, began teaching law, and married Bill Clinton in 1975.

In 1980, she was made a senior litigating partner at the prestigious Rose Law Firm in Little Rock. She gave birth to her only daughter, Chelsea, the same month she was made partner. She went on to be appointed director of three major corporate boards, and on two of them, the TCBY yogurt company and the retail giant Wal-Mart, was the first woman ever to gain membership. She pushed Wal-Mart to revamp its hiring and promotion practices for women and minorities, and was instrumental in leading the company into taking more aggressive environmental-protection actions.

The woman her friends describe as fun and funny, intensely loyal, passionate and caring, never planned on being the first lady of the United States. Her first wish was to be an astronaut. But NASA told her to take her dreams elsewhere, so she turned her sights instead on the law. Her mother was sure she'd make it to the Supreme Court. Her law school friends thought they'd see her elected to office. Her husband wanted to put her in his Cabinet.

"I want to be a voice for children in the White House" is the last thing she's said on the matter.

"I don't have any personal ambitions," Hillary told a local reporter a few years ago. "I just think you should have some fun with your life and not take yourself real seriously." Her life to date has proven those two statements if not untrue than seriously insufficient. It is true that her ambitions have never, since the time she moved to Arkansas, existed independently of Bill Clinton's overarching political dreams. But now, as she steps into her most important position, it is hard to know if she will be playing a supporting or a principal role in the White House.

In 1987, when Bill Clinton considered running for president—but didn't—Hillary was asked by the *Arkansas Gazette* what she thought it would feel like to be personally embroiled in a presidential race. "It has to be impossible even to imagine what it means," she said then. "You could maybe sit here and intellectualize it, but to experience it has to be of a totally different quality."

The race has come and gone, and Hillary Clinton has found out—the hard way—what twelve months in the public fray means. Now it's time to put that knowledge to work. It's time to discover what first ladyship means. Hillary Rodham Clinton, having climbed the ladder to professional success, has just completed the most difficult assignment of her life. She is now the most powerful woman in the United States. The most powerful woman in the world. What will she do with that power? What kind of first lady will she be? It's time these questions were answered. And there's no better place to start than in looking at who she's been up until now.

1

Hillary Rodham

In the early 1950s, Park Ridge, Illinois, was the kind of place where parents dreamed of moving and children loved to live. Hugh and Dorothy Rodham were parents with dreams, and highest among them was to make their children happy. A few years after the war, joining the mass migration of Americans fleeing crowded cities, they took the plunge into the suburbs. Hugh was a salesman working hard at building his own small textile business. Dorothy was a stay-at-home mother with great hopes for her family, especially for her smart preschool girl, Hillary. Park Ridge, then as now, was mostly a bedroom community consisting of families whose fathers or mothers commuted to Chicago daily. Most had moved to the suburb, which had been incorporated only a few decades earlier, in the 1940s and 1950s. They were drawn by the promise of excellent schools, densely tree-lined streets, gaslight-style streetlamps shining over stone-engraved street signs, and family-sized houses ranging from modest to sub-

stantial. The town did boast, though, several landmark
buildings, in the central Uptown area, such as the Pick-
wick Theater. There was only one relatively major an-
noyance: "I grew up," Hillary once joked, "under
flight patterns at O'Hare Airport."

The Rodhams were not particularly bothered. They
hadn't chosen Park Ridge as a real estate investment—
though their yellow brick house on Wisner Road really
was nice. It was a large Georgian-style home with tall
trees out front and a well-tended yard. It was a big,
comfortable house, surrounded by others just like it,
on a quiet street with neighbors just like them. Families
left their doors unlocked, and children considered one
anothers' backyards their own. All through the neighborhood, children ran from house to house, rode their
bikes in circles down the middle of quiet streets, or
pedaled off for a ride down bigger boulevards, where
the older trees formed a canopy over their heads.

The Rodham family, five strong, well off but not
rich, solid in their bonds, fit in well in the neighborhood. Methodists of Welsh and English descent, they
blended in easily in a community that was, above all,
homogeneous. It was a conservative community,
home of later antiabortion fighters Henry Hyde and
Penny Pullen, filled with dyed-in-the-wool Republicans and a few John Birchers too. It was also, not coincidentally, a dry town, although liquor was sold just
one township over, and road trips out and deliveries in
were frequent enough that any white panel truck that
crossed the city line and pulled into a private alleyway
was immediately considered suspect.

But the most important thing that the families of
Park Ridge had in common was an unflagging belief in
education. They were themselves a highly educated,
upper-middle-class group, and they wanted their chil-

dren to do even better. They were even willing to pay for it.

"I've often kidded my father, who has never been a fan of taxes or government, about moving to a place that had such high property taxes to pay for school," Hillary told Bill Clinton's biographer, Charles F. Allen. "But even though it was a very conservative Republican community, there was just no griping during the fifties and sixties about paying for good education."

Starting when they were very young, both Rodhams worked hard to instill the sense in Hillary and her two brothers, Hugh and Tony, that the biggest responsibility of their young lives was to be sure they got the best education possible. "Learning for learning's sake," her mother said. "Learning for earning's sake," her father joked.

Dorothy Rodham herself had not gone to college. She had married Hugh, a Pennsylvania State University graduate, and devoted her life to him and their children. She turned her kind heart and rich intelligence to child-rearing, and she seemed at peace with her life. But she promised herself that her daughter would have more options. Her daughter, she swore, would never be so unsure of her knowledge that she would drop out of conversations, or simply play supportive audience to her husband's stronger voice. Her daughter, she swore, would be able to *say* and *do* anything she wanted.

"I was determined that no daughter of mine was going to have to go through the agony of being afraid to say what she had on her mind," she said. "Just because she was a girl didn't mean she should be limited. . . . I don't know whether you could say that was unusual at the time," she explained to a reporter from the *Washington Post*. "I guess it was more of an accepted role to stay within your own scope."

Hillary's scope, Dorothy decided, would be as wide and dream-filled as possible. It would be as big as Hillary's belief in herself could make it. As she said in an interview with the French magazine *Paris Match*, "I explained to her very early that school was a great adventure . . . that she was going to learn great things, live new passions. I motivated her in a way that she wasn't 'resigned' to go to school. I wanted her to be excited by the idea. Maybe that's why Hillary was never afraid. Not of school. Not of anything."

As Hillary recalled many years later: "[My parents] told me that it was my obligation to go to school, that I had an obligation to use my mind. They told me that an education would enable me to have a lot more opportunities in life, that if I went to school and took it seriously and studied hard, not only would I learn things and become interested in the world around me, but I would open up all kinds of doors to myself so that when I was older I would have some control over my environment. It was education for education's sake," she told the *Arkansas Democrat*, "but also it was the idea that school was a real pathway to a better opportunity."

Fortunately, Hillary didn't need much prodding. As a student she, along with every other school child in America, watched with an almost personal dismay as the Russians launched the first Sputnik rocket into space. In her first public-service-minded move, she swore that she'd devote herself to science. "When Hillary started school," Dorothy Rodham remembered, "from the time she was five on, she was told that the Russians had sent the first satellite into space. She reacted like all the other children. Like their parents too. That race to go into space was so important to our way of thinking that America couldn't tolerate that the Russians had gotten ahead of us. To catch up, there was only one choice: to learn, to gain knowledge, and to invent. I think that it was following that historical event and the reaction it provoked that our children developed that hunger for learning, that desire to become competent in every field."

Home life taught Hillary that she could do anything and everything. "I felt very fortunate because as a girl growing up I never felt anything but support from my family," she later explained to Charles Allen. "Whatever I thought I could do or be, they supported. There was no distinction between me and my brothers or any barriers thrown up to me that I couldn't think about doing something because I was a girl. It was just: if you work hard enough and you really apply yourself, then you should be able to do whatever you choose to do."

Although home, and her parents' gentle nudging, gave Hillary a sense of unlimited possibility, the outside world wasn't quite so encouraging. While she was still in junior high school, she decided she wanted to be an astronaut. It was the early 1960s and the nation, under President Kennedy's leadership, was thinking moonwards. Hillary wrote to NASA and asked them what she needed to do to start training. She included some mention of her background and academic strengths. NASA wrote back telling her that girls need not apply. It was, she said, "infuriating." She told the *Washington Post*: "I later realized that I couldn't have been an astronaut anyway, because I have such terrible eyesight. That somewhat placated me."

Hillary had too much of a support base at home, though, to be stopped in her tracks so quickly. Her father, a man whose business occupied most of his waking hours, was, in his more reserved way, as great a supporter of his daughter's prodigious skills as his wife.

"It really was the classic parenting situation, where

the mother is the encourager and the helper, and the father brings news from the outside world," Hillary said in an interview with *Glamour*. "The role fathers play in empowering girls is critical." Her own father's style lay in fostering a pragmatic competitiveness. Without putting his daughter down, he let her know that there was always much more to be achieved. "My father would come home and say, 'You did well, but could you do better? It's hard out there.' Encouragement was tempered with realism."

Hugh Rodham's method, which might have seemed unduly tough for a less hardy soul than Hillary, was based on real concern. He had attended Penn State on a football scholarship, and knew how close he had come to not receiving a higher education. He didn't want his daughter ever to run that risk.

"My parents set really high expectations for me and were rarely satisfied," Hillary told the *Democrat*. "I would come home from school with a good grade, and my father would say, 'Must have been an easy assignment.' "

Her spirit, though, was unbreakable. "I always felt challenged. I always felt as though there was something else out there I could reach for," she said.

Outside of school, Hillary threw herself into developing new talents and hobbies with the determination of a budding perfectionist. Her brothers kept pretty busy too. Dorothy Rodham found herself stuck in the suburban mom's role of chauffeur. As she told *Paris Match*, "I spent all my time in the car then; I had three children and each one had his or her little activity. I always encouraged them to do what they wanted to do. So I spent my time driving back and forth across town."

Like a dutiful daughter of the upper-middle class, Hillary studied music and dance. At age ten, she was already in toe shoes, a sturdy child, proud of her pink ballet tights and tutu, with straight dark blonde hair falling long down her back. Her piano lessons were slightly less successful. "She had a wonderful teacher," her mother recalled, "but she drove herself and him to desperation because she was only able to play with one hand!"

Though the Rodham household was financially comfortable, and Dorothy was home all the time, she made sure her boys and daughter did not grow up spoiled. She particularly did not want little Hillary turning into a privileged princess. "She was never paid for the chores she did around the house like some parents pay their children, a dollar for mowing the lawn, another for washing the car," Dorothy Rodham told *Paris Match*. "As my husband always said, 'They eat and sleep for free! We're not going to pay them for it as well!' "

From a very early age Hillary was encouraged to earn her own money. She started baby-sitting when she was herself little more than a child, helped out in a day-care center, and, when she was slightly older, worked as salesperson in a store. Vacations were spent in similarly renumerative activity. Dorothy did not encourage sloth. She had big plans for her daughter, and she figured that a sense of responsibility couldn't hurt. She told her so too.

"I've always spoken to Hillary as you would to an adult," she said. "I think that parents now speak like that to their children, but then it was the opposite. You considered them only children and didn't try to make them understand. I never did that."

Hillary Rodham spent her first three years of high school at Maine East High, the alma mater of Harrison Ford, and then was redistricted to the newly built Maine South her senior year. High school was an eye-opening experience for her. For the first time she shared classes with students from suburbs beyond Park Ridge. There were working-class kids from Skokie, Catholics and Jews, and even some recent immigrants from abroad. Unlike many of her classmates, Hillary went out of her way to befriend the newcomers.

"Hillary always liked to hang out with as many different groups of people as she could," recalls Sherry Heiden, a geneticist and a good friend from that era. "She always had a really broad view of people; she was never a narrow person."

All Hillary's good efforts, however, did not change the fact that the school's suburban integration efforts did not extend to bringing in blacks. "It was a lily-white area," Heiden remembers. "I think finally by our senior year there was one black kid in the whole school."

Enter Don Jones, currently a professor of religion at Drew University in New Jersey. At the time Hillary was a freshman, Jones was fresh out of the Drew University Theological School, and he had been assigned to the Rodhams' church, First Methodist, for his first job as a youth minister. That assignment would prove one of the most formative experiences in young Hillary Rodham's life.

"We were just getting out of the Eisenhower era, the Pat Boone era, the passive period, and moving into the revolutionary decade where so many things would happen," Jones recalls. "Kennedy had just been elected, and the civil rights laws would be passed within two years. That's when I first got in touch with Hillary."

Her friends were too young then to drive cars and weren't even allowed into downtown Chicago without their parents. Jones took the youth group on trips into the inner city. They visited a recreation center in one of the city's toughest neighborhoods and met with black gangs and Hispanic groups. Under Jones's leadership, Hillary and some of the other high school girls began to organize baby-sitting brigades for the children of migrant workers who were living in what were then farm lands not far to the west and south of Park Ridge.

"He just was relentless in telling us that to be a Christian did not just mean you were concerned about your own personal salvation," Hillary told *Newsweek*.

"I don't think those kids had seen poverty before. I don't think they had interacted with kids that weren't like themselves," Jones says. "Religion, going to church, tended to function there for most people to reinforce their rather traditional conservative values. And so when I came in and took that white middle-class youth group into the inner city of Chicago, that was quite radical."

At Drew, Jones had studied under the esteemed theologian Paul Tillich and had been exposed to creative new methods of relating theology to art and culture. He took these teachings with him to Park Ridge, where he exposed the high school kids to Picasso, e. e. cummings, and Stephen Crane. While some played the guitar, the group sang folk songs, Bob Dylan songs, then talked about the lyrics. Jones screened films like *Requiem for a Heavyweight* and *The 400 Blows*.

"I took a print of Picasso's *Guernica*, took it into the inner city, set it on the back of a chair, and asked both groups, the city group and the suburban group, to look at that painting and not say anything, and then we talked about it in terms of their experience. I asked them if it reminded them of anything, even what kind of music they would set it to—just to even out the playing field, so as not to give a discursive advantage to the better-educated kids. I might ask them simple things like: what strikes you, what grabs you? Some kids would say, the baby and the mother crying and wailing, or the broken arm, or the light bulb in the middle. And then I would say things like: did this remind you of any experience you've had? What was interesting was that the inner-city kids were able to relate to the tragic dimensions of that painting better than the suburban kids. I remember one girl from Chicago started crying and said, 'Why did my uncle have to die just because he parked in the wrong parking place?' And she started to tell us that just three days before, her uncle had parked in the wrong place and some guy pulled out a gun and said that's my parking place, and they got into an argument and the guy shot her uncle."

Sherry Heiden, who was a member of Hillary's youth group, recalls those inner-city visits as part and parcel of the golden age of the early sixties, when hope was still on the rise and drugs had not yet come to infiltrate the schools. "It was a time when a lot of the idealism that was going to fuel the sixties and early seventies was becoming known about. We believed in the incredible social changes that can happen if you change your perspective."

A high point for Hillary came in 1962 when, through Don Jones, she met Dr. Martin Luther King, Jr. He was addressing a Sunday Evening Club meeting, a weekly event that drew preachers from around the country to give talks in Orchestra Hall in downtown Chicago. After King's talk, Jones took his youth group backstage. He stood next to King and introduced the teenagers to him one by one. Hillary Rodham's eyes were shining as she shook his hand.

Hillary started dropping by Jones's office at the church frequently. In the afternoons after school. She liked to talk about ideas. "She was intellectual even then," he says. "She was open-minded. She was curious, open to what life had to bring. When I introduced her to a lot of new things, she was just insatiable." Jones introduced Hillary, in small doses, to the difficult theological writings of Dietrich Bonhoeffer, Reinhold Niebuhr, and Paul Tillich. Then he decided to present her with a different kind of challenge.

He reached back from his desk and took a small paperback book off his bookshelf.

"Here," he said, "you ought to read this. And we'll talk about it later."

Hillary glanced at the book jacket. It was J. D. Salinger's *Catcher in the Rye*, a scandalous book in those days.

"She read the book, but she didn't say much about it, so I didn't say much about it," Jones recalls. "But in college she had to read it again for an English class, and she wrote a letter to me her sophomore year that said, 'I didn't tell you at the time, but when you had me read *Catcher in the Rye*, I didn't like it, and moreover, I thought it was a little too advanced for me. But now that I've read it the second time, I realize, I think, why you gave that to me. I don't think it was too advanced, as a matter of fact.' " She then admitted just how much Holden Caufield reminded her of her younger brother Hugh.

Hugh Rodham was a few years younger than Hillary, but he already was causing his family some trouble. Nothing serious. He just wasn't the perfect child that his sister was.

"Hughie was kind of a rascal," Jones says. "A roustabout. I think I played some role in taming him."

(Hugh Rodham went on to play quarterback for Coach Joe Paterno at Penn State and is now a highly respected public defender in Miami.)

Jones's reassignment to another church was an end of an era at the Youth Ministry. Though he and Hillary kept in touch by letters, the new pastor was cut of quite a different cloth. "He thinks I'm a radical," Hillary wrote to Jones.

But she too was entering into a new stage in her life, preparing for college. She was also living out the highs and lows of a high school social life. The rules of the game didn't at first come naturally to her.

"I saw a lot of my friends who had been really lively and smart and doing well in school beginning to worry that boys would think they were too smart, or beginning to cut back on how well they did or the courses they took, because that's not where their boyfriends were," Hillary explained to the *Washington Post*. "And I can recall thinking, 'Gosh, why are they doing that?' It didn't make sense to me."

It didn't interest her all that much either. She marched to the beat of her own drummer, dressing as she liked, wearing glasses, prioritizing studying over worrying about her next date. "Hillary was never style-conscious," Dorothy Rodham told the fashion magazine *W.* "She didn't have to have what her peers had."

Her indifference to flirting and fashion didn't mean she wasn't popular with boys, however—far from it.

"Boys liked her," Jones says. "And not because she was flirtatious. She was not—she wasn't a raving beauty, but she was pretty enough. What attracted guys around her was her personality, her willingness to talk to them, at parity with them."

As a child, Hillary had literally fought her way to parity with the neighborhood boys. As Gail Sheehy tells the story, there was a little girl in her neighborhood named Suzy who enjoyed spending afternoons beating Hillary into tears. Hillary, a rather even-tempered child, didn't get it at first. But after she came home crying a few too many times, her mother encouraged her to get mad and strike back.

"There's no room in this house for cowards," she said. "You'll have to stand up to her. The next time she hits you, I want you to hit her back."

Hillary took the advice and went back out. She was instantly surrounded by her tormentor and a circle of boys. Suddenly, without thinking, she struck out, and Suzy was knocked down. Charged with victory, Hillary ran home and told her mother, "I can play with the boys now!"

"Boys responded well to Hillary," her mother concluded. "She just took charge, and they let her."

Sometimes Hillary's ease in attracting boys didn't endear her to female friends. On a vacation trip that Hillary took in high school with some friends, she ran into a problem when one young woman, eager to meet boys, struck out, while Hillary, without even trying, ended up surrounded by a small circle of followers. One night, after she'd sat out on the front porch with a new male acquaintance and talked until past midnight, she came in to bed and found her friend seething with rage. It didn't do much for her sense of female solidarity.

Most of the time, though, Hillary hung around a large group of friends, both male and female. Among them was the folk singer Steve Goodman. They went to football and basketball games, and to school dances afterward, and to restaurants. There wasn't much by way of drugs around, in the early sixties, and no alcohol. Her friends were high achievers like herself, and not likely to be getting into trouble with parents or the law. Most times the friends would gather in the home of Hillary's friend Betsy Johnson, fifteen or twenty strong, and sit around, eat, watch television, and talk. One-on-one dating was rare.

Hillary organized circuses and amateur sports tournaments to raise money for migrant workers. She participated in a school talent show with Steve Goodman and her friend and long-time admirer Rick Ricketts, and scolded them for not rehearsing enough. She had an incredible talent for rallying high school boys to do her service-oriented bidding.

"She always had the energy and the drive and the ability to size people up and know who was going to be able to work hard, and who was just doing it for reasons other than real dedication," Sherry Heiden laughed.

She went ice skating and skiing and tobaggoning with the youth group. And she played softball. She loved team sports. In those pre-Title VII school days, though, there were no girls' athletics teams. Girls who wanted to excel outside of the academic arena were advised instead to get into the school clubs and student government. Which is just what she did.

Hillary became a senior leader—a sort of assistant teacher—in her last year of high school. She was also chairman of the organization committee, a thankless and somewhat frustrating job that made her responsible for getting up in front of the 2,700-student body and running the school assemblies. She was vice president of her junior class and a member of the national honor society. She graduated in the top five percent of her class. She was the girl voted most likely to succeed by her senior class. (The boy in her class voted most likely to succeed died of a drug overdose four years later.) At her graduation, she won so many awards that, Dorothy Rodham told *People*, "it was embarrassing."

Clearly, high school was the start of something.

"You looked at Hillary and, you know, she wanted to be a lawyer, she was going to be a lawyer, anything she wanted to be, she was going to do it. She was always really motivated," said a classmate, Michael Andrews, who is now a math teacher at Main South.

She was also showing the early signs of the talent for negotiation and conciliation that would come to define her activist work in college and law school. "She was a forceful person, confident, obviously motivated, and she was able to get things done. She was active and she was a leader. The kids just kind of automatically looked up to her because she spoke out for things that she believed in. She would take an unpopular stance on something and would be willing to be in the minority position, and be able to support that position," recalls Kenneth Reese, Hillary's driver's-ed teacher and student council coordinator during her senior year.

"It wasn't a matter of her being a rebel in any sense. It was just that she was confident in her own skills—she was bright and had strong convictions and was able to follow through on them," Reese says. "She saw all the sides of an issue, and she was able to integrate those and then make a judgment. The kids respected her. They respect somebody who has strong leadership skills and can articulate issues."

"I think another reason they looked up to her too was because she was really interested in them and what they were doing," recalls Ann Finneran, a physical education teacher at Main South for whom Hillary worked as a senior leader. "She wasn't one of those people who stand off and think they're better than everybody else. She liked people a lot."

The importance of Dorothy Rodham's influence on Hillary Clinton's early education cannot be overestimated. She instilled in her daughter the sense of the unlimited possibilities of learning—and of her own limitless potential. And she believed in herself too. Sherry Heiden remembers that Mrs. Rodham was the only mother she knew who started taking community college courses "just for the thrill of it, just to do something with her mind" in her free time.

"Dorothy was a big influence on Hillary. She has such an interest in the world and such an interest in people's minds," Heiden says.

Her mother provided Hillary with a model for self-esteem.

This quality comes through in every yearbook picture taken of her that senior spring. In each shot she looks like someone with forward-looking dreams. In group pictures she is always seated front and center, hands neatly folded in her lap, her eyes locked in the camera's gaze. Her clothing is carefully chosen, and it is almost pre-Ann Taylor in style: houndstooth skirt, sleeveless blouse, sensibly high-heeled shoes. Her hair is smartly bobbed and curled under. She has an intensity that the other students lack. A presence.

In choosing to go east to Wellesley College, Hillary did stand out from her classmates. Most students from Park Ridge were attending local colleges. According to Kenneth Reese, going to Wellesley was seen as "adventurous and cosmopolitan."

It was really more adventurous than Reese had thought. Hillary had chosen Wellesley on an impulse. Her senior year she had had two young teachers who were studying for their master's degrees in education at Northwestern and had been assigned to teach in her school. One of them had graduated from Wellesley, the other from Smith College. "They were both so bright and smart and terrific teachers, and they lobbied me so hard to apply to these schools which I had never thought of before," she explained to Charles Allen. "And then when I was accepted, they lobbied me hard to go and be able to work out all of the financial and other issues associated with it. So I went to Wellesley."

The Wellesley campus had, she noted, looked very pretty in photographs. It seemed elegant—and intimidating too. But Hillary wouldn't stay intimidated for long.

The 1960s, Hillary Rodham once said, were "years dominated by men with dreams, men in the civil rights movement and the Peace Corps, the space program." She came to Wellesley, one of the finest, most progressive women's colleges in the country, intent upon finding her place in that men's world of social progress. Wellesley was then the right place to do it.

"There was a sense of coming of age on campus then," a classmate recalls. "A sense of empowerment."

Hillary arrived at college a Park Ridge Republican with box-pleat skirts, Peter Pan blouses, and loafers with knee socks. In high school she had gone door-to-door canvassing for Goldwater; now the former Goldwater Girl became president of the Young Republicans. She was an outspoken opponent of big government and high taxes, and, though her heart bled for the poor, she believed in self-reliance and in the responsibility of local governments to look after their own. All of that changed, though, rather quickly.

When she began college in the fall of 1965, the Goldwater-Johnson election, in which she had spoken out for the right wing with all the passion of a teenager, was becoming ancient history. A great deal had happened in the world during the last six months of her senior high school year. Dr. Martin Luther King, Jr., had led the march on Selma, Alabama. For the first time northerners had seen fire hoses and police dogs raining hate on African Americans down South. Hillary Rodham, who only two years before had shook Dr. King's hand, saw white policemen in storm trooper boots using cattle prods on peaceful black and white demonstrators, saw federal troops called in to keep the peace. Such images did not fail to make a mark on her.

Hillary majored in political science and also studied psychology. Her mentor was a professor named Alan Schechter, a liberal, open-minded man with a passion for the subject of civil rights and a group of young students eager to share in that passion. They studied together through the assassinations of Martin Luther King, Jr., and Robert F. Kennedy, the fall of Malcolm X and the Black Panthers, the Weathermen, the Vietnam War and the protests. "We had the assassinations of the leaders, we had the loss of hope and expectations about progress, we had the war and all the teach-ins," Schechter recalls. "It really was a moment in American history that was unique in terms of problems confronting society."

"We were in school when everything seemed to be falling apart at the seams," says Kris Olson Rogers, a college friend who is now dean and Professor of Law at the Northwestern School of Law at Lewis and Clark University. "And the campus often reflected the unrest in society at large."

Hillary certainly did. In the course of her first year, she became radicalized—to a point. She adopted the horn-rimmed glasses, granny skirts, and muslin dresses de rigeur at the time. Her academic career became a search for "relevance." She edged her way leftward through the moderate Rockefeller wing of the Republican party and by 1968 was campaigning for the Democrat Eugene McCarthy, thinking about women's issues, and talking about minority rights and the needs of the poor.

"There was a sea of change in Hillary," recalls Jeff Shields, a Chicago attorney who dated her while he was a student at Harvard. "There was a great deal of change going on in the country and she reflected some of it."

Shields, who began dating Hillary during the first semester of her freshman year, recalls her transformation from someone unsure in her views to a competent political thinker who loved nothing more than a good debate. "In the first while that I knew Hillary, she tended to listen more than talk," he remembers. "But as time went by, she solidified her beliefs. We spent lots of time with friends sitting around coffee tables in somebody's suites, having a beer or a Coke and talking in an animated way about politics and government and societal issues. There were lots of animated discussions on civil rights, civil liberties issues, and international issues—particularly in the Southeast Asia context."

Hillary, according to Shields, always seemed to have a political mission—even before she had a vision to go with it. "From the first time I met her, I remember being struck by her real interest in government from the point of view of someone who wanted to be involved and have an impact, but didn't know exactly how," he says. "She didn't have fixed ambitions in terms of knowing that she wanted to be elected to some office, and she certainly didn't give any indication that she was looking to attach herself to a politician—and I'm sure probably would have been offended by that concept if someone had raised it at that time."

Some friends say that the actual philosophical change that went on in Hillary Rodham's mind during college has been exaggerated. Her early support for Goldwater in Park Ridge and Young Republicanism was a last gasp of unconscious childhood parent-miming, they say, stressing that Hillary never was a hard-core conservative.

"Most of her thinking seemed to be based, as all of

ours was based, on her parents' perspective," her friend and political comrade-in-arms Eleanor "Eldee" Acheson recalls. Acheson, who came from a liberal, highly political family, welcomed her classmate's shift to the left. In the fall of 1968, she drove her around the state as the two young women campaigned for Senator Hubert Humphrey, doing literature drops and phone banks in Massachusetts and New Hampshire. "I never got into a conversation with her in which I thought that she held conservative views that would translate into being discriminatory about blacks or Catholics or Jews or anybody. I don't remember that kind of substantive conservatism."

Acheson grew close to Hillary in a constitutional law seminar they both took their senior year. It was taught by Professor Schechter, one of a new breed of teachers in the humanities and social sciences who led classroom discussions with an eye to advocacy-oriented ways of teaching. Acheson, a sharp, strong-minded history major, found herself drawn to her smart, intense classmate with the big light-up smile, who wore thick, heavy-rimmed glasses like her own and flopped her long hair negligently into a clip at the back of her neck.

"She was not one of those know-it-alls who lectured people and lectured the professor and answered everything in the context of their political beliefs," she says. "She asked fabulously insightful questions and then used the avenue opened up by the questions as a way to pursue points and issues."

"She was never strident about what her beliefs were," says Dana Stambaugh Semeraro, Hillary's Wellesley "big sister." "She was always so enthusiastic that she inspired other people to follow her. She was unlike a lot of people who are dedicated to causes and become rather offensive and rather condescending if you're not involved in these causes at the same level of energy. She was a down-to-earth person, she had a great sense of humor, and people liked her."

Hillary and Eldee Acheson spoke frequently and passionately about the issues that interested them, often stopping to greet each other rapidly on the steps of Founders Hall between classes and talking until they were both late for class. "When you ran into her, you could just say hi and pass by, but if you wanted to stop and talk about something, you could really find yourself drawn into it more than you thought," Acheson says. "She was the sort of the way she is now: a lot of fun, with a great sense of humor, but not a frivolous person in the least. So if you stopped and said, have you read this or that article, next thing you knew she'd read it and she'd read about ten other articles and was kind of rolling away in conversation. And it was very substantive, she was very connected."

Acheson, Hillary, and a handful of friends settled in nearby rooms in the modern dormitory complex Stone-Davis, which became known as the place where student leaders lived. They were a group of earthy, intense, committed, politically active young women. Almost all were from relatively conservative, upper-middle-class backgrounds like Hillary's, and almost all were struggling through breaking with the political preferences of their parents.

"I would describe us all as typically earnest students of the late sixties: idealists, thinking that maybe one person could make a differnce," recalls Kris Rogers.

It was a sylvan setting for study: tall trees, elegant New England landscaping, stone Gothic buildings, a windowed dining room overlooking the foliage for long dinners with friends. In the Stone-Davis dorm common area, Hillary was often found in the evenings holding a sort of social issues *salon*, surrounded by

wildly debating friends discussing the issues of the day
or plotting the early stages of yet another push for college reform. Hillary's exceptional skills as a leader
made her stand out. "Hillary was definitely one of a
handful of leaders," Rogers says. "But she was the one
who was always giving speeches, calling meetings,
making things happen. She was a catalyst."

The first-year students weren't allowed to have cars,
go away for the weekends without parental permission, or have boys in their rooms, so when weekends
came, they took the nearby Green Line train to Boston,
where they knocked around the bookstores and cafés
of Harvard Square. There were mixers around Harvard
and some co-registration with the men at MIT, but it
wasn't a roaring social scene. "The biggest social life
on campus was tea on Wednesday afternoon, you
know, one lump or two," Rogers says.

Hillary Rodham met Jeff Shields when she went out
on a date with his roommate. She dated him through
the first half of her senior year at Wellesley, along with
a number of other men—all of whom, according to
Rogers, were "poli-sci, earnest-idealist, policy-activist,
good-government types, not wild-eyed radicals."

Shields, a Harvard student two years ahead of her,
remembers Hillary as a serious, active, and intellectual
young woman who knew how to have fun but primarily spent her time living, breathing, and talking politics.

She took him on long walks around the lake at
Wellesley, talking all the while. He followed. "She listened to what people were thinking about and were
interested in reading, and then she'd read that author's work and come back and be able to discuss it."
After a few turns around the lake, Hillary gave Shields
a copy of Thoreau's *Walden*. They also discussed Locke
and the early political philosophers.

"It was a relationship based on a lot of discourse," he says.

But Rodham and Shields did stop talking politics once in a while. They went to football games and dances and private parties in the suites of Winthrop House, his Harvard dorm. Hillary was outgoing and could chat with anyone. She also loved to dance and was good at it too. They danced to the Beatles and Motown. Hillary particularly liked the Supremes.

The image of the dance-loving, gregarious Hillary tends to be the one that Alan Schechter carries with him in his mind. "She was not overly bookish, or interested in grades, or committed to studying too hard," he says. "She was a warm, friendly, outgoing, smiling, relaxed person."

She was a pretty young woman too, with straight blond hair hanging loosely down to her shoulders and a slim, athletic physique. But she wasn't the type to spend Friday afternoons agonizing over her looks for an evening at Harvard. "She was not a woman who spent a lot of time thinking of how she looked or what she wore," a classmate recalls.

She was a uniquely loyal friend, the type who would put herself out on a limb to see that no one else suffered unnecessarily, and that justice, to the best of her abilities, was always done. "She didn't just take things that happened and accept them," the classmate says. "She fulfilled some of the community's obligation to gather a group together and bring about change."

While other Wellesley women buried themselves in the library, or spent their time mooning over faraway boyfriends or on-campus intrigues, Hillary kept herself active in student government and off-campus activities.

She followed a rigorous schedule. She made frequent trips into the Roxbury section of Boston, where

she worked teaching poor children to read. Boston
then was embroiled in controversies over voting access
for blacks. Hillary and her friends got involved in
working on an alternative newspaper in the black community and participated in inter-campus activist
groups with Harvard and MIT.

Wellesley, like the nation, was then embarking on a
period of change. In Hillary's freshman year, the greatest number of black students ever admitted had entered the school. They formed the campus' first African American women's association, and took on the
university, charging that a secret quota policy was being used to keep their numbers down. There were talks
of strikes and other political action. A campus-wide
meeting was called in the Wellesley chapel. Hillary
presided.

Facilitating and conciliating among all the groups,
she kept channels of communications open and built
bridges, assembled coalitions of groups, and served as
a liaison between those groups and the administration
once issues became polarized. "She did a sort of shut-
tle diplomacy among all the groups," Kris Rogers says.
"She had a talent for serving as a bridge between different groups of students. She tried to keep everybody
talking and figured out a way to move the institution
out of its inertia and also accommodate the concerns of
black students."

Rogers suggests that it was precisely Hillary's not-
long-distant conservatism that made her such a natural
mediator. "As she evolved personally into more Democratic politics, I think Hillary was able to not close off
those channels of communication from her earlier
roots. She definitely gained from them an empathy for
various segments of the population who very often in
those days weren't speaking to each other at all."

As a junior, Hillary became a counselor responsible

for working with freshmen in her dorm. She also worked her way up through the ranks of campus government. She joined in the fight to loosen parietal restrictions and helped lead protests against Wellesley's rigid academic distribution requirements and for a pass-fail grading system. As president of the college government her senior year, she organized the first set of teach-ins on the Vietnam War on campus. Reports of the war's escalation were quickly turning concern into outrage, and campus attitudes toward the war were growing more violent. The goal originally had been for the teach-ins to be educational rather than polemic. But dominant anti-war feeling among the students soon turned them into protests.

These were mild, however, compared to the anti-war activities at other schools in the fall of 1968. Wellesley students, in an all-women college, were not subject to the firsthand pains of the draft. There was no ROTC chapter or CIA recruiters coming around. Protest remained an academic, intellectual concern, not a matter of civil disobedience, and certainly nothing that would stand in the way of any liberal, pragmatic, ambitiously career-minded young woman's future.

Hillary Rodham was that kind of young woman. She was, according to Alan Schechter, a "pragmatic liberal who believed in what I call instrumental liberalism: using government to meet the unmet needs of the society to help those people who are not fully included within it."

She wrote her senior thesis on a comparative study of community-action programs for the poor, analyzing them to determine the conditions under which the participation of the poor in taking control of their lives could have a lasting positive impact. Her conclusion was that on a short-term basis, participation of the poor in trying to improve their lives would help them, but the betterment would be temporary. Broader programs with more sustained help were needed to achieve longer-term impact. She received A's from all four of her thesis graders.

"It was a liberal, progressive kind of thesis, but in no sense a radical one," says Schechter, who served as her thesis adviser. "She was progressive but critical. Pragmatic. Exactly the way she's pursued her whole subsequent professional career."

Just as Hillary never really had positioned herself all that far to the right, her swing leftward stopped just left of center. "She was really very mainstream," Jeff Shields says. "She was not a counterculture person. I never got the sense from her that it was likely that she was going to drop out or become radical, even in her thinking, because even when she became definitively liberal, it was always within a fairly conventional scope."

Perhaps the most important course Hillary took at Wellesley was Schechter's constitutional law seminar during her last year there. Once a week the small group of seniors would meet, sit in a circle, and hash out the issues of the day. Many of them were involved in the anti-Vietnam movement, some, like Hillary, had worked on Eugene McCarthy's campaign; others, like Eldee Acheson had worked for Bobby Kennedy. They were unhappy with the course that the country was taking. They saw their brothers, cousins, and boyfriends going off to war. They felt the government was out of touch. They were involved and committed, and believed that the fact of being college students in the late 1960s was itself of historical importance. And they were frustrated with the fact that at their graduation, no one would be there to talk about their shared history.

"We need a class speaker, one of us," someone decided. Hillary and Eldee Acheson agreed. With Schechter's coaching and encouragement, they took the idea to Wellesley President Ruth Adams. She, not surprisingly, said no.

The constitutional law scholars made their case. They took the idea to the student body, and it was enthusiastically approved. Then they set about finding a speaker who would go over well with the administration. A good student, a class leader, a popular woman who they could honestly say spoke for the class. They settled on Hillary Rodham. She was a natural choice—president of student government, a straight-A honors student, well-known and popular on campus. Having been a go-between for so long between so many groups, she was one of the only women whom everyone could claim as a fair representative of their interests.

The administration agreed. Wellesley President Adams specified only that the speaker's remarks were to reflect a consensus of the graduating class, and that her remarks be "appropriate" and not embarrass the college. In a "consensus" style typical of the day, Hillary opened the speechwriting process to suggestions from her classmates. They deluged her with ideas, poems, quotations. They wanted her to talk about what they had seen in the past four years, they said: the escalation of the Vietnam War, the assassinations of Martin Luther King and Bobby Kennedy, and the riots in the cities. A small committee of speechwriters, including Acheson, sifted through the ideas and came up with a tentative draft.

A few days before commencement, Adams demanded the right to review the speech. Acheson and friends refused, making arguments against prior restraint. They delivered a final draft of the speech to Hillary, who made her final changes.

At that time it was traditional for the administration to invite an outside speaker to graduation. And in Hillary's year the chosen speaker was Senator Edward Brooke, a liberal Republican from Massachusetts. The commencement scheduler, clearly not anticipating a war of words from the pulpit, scheduled Brooke to speak right before Hillary. It was an unfortunate mistake.

Many prominent guests came that day. Eldee Acheson's grandfather, Dean Acheson, former secretary of state under Truman, was there with his wife. Paul Nitze, who had been deputy secretary of defense during the Vietnam War, was there for his daughter Nina. Other prominent people from business, the financial world and government were in attendance, drawing more press coverage than usual.

Senator Brooke spoke for his allotted time without incident. And without substance, many of Hillary's classmates believed. "It was pretty much a canned speech, full of highfalutin words and concepts, but it could have been given anywhere, anyplace, anytime," Eldee Acheson says. "He did not weave into its ideas or its content or its message anything about the four years we had spent at that school and what had happened to the country in those four years. It was totally vapid."

After he finished speaking, Hillary Rodham approached the pulpit. She looked small and rather young in her oversized cap and gown. She faced her classmates, her parents, the board of trustees, and the reunited alumnae. Then she began.

Senator Brooke's remarks, she said, reflected just the kind of disconnected, irrelevant thinking that had led the country astray for four years. "I find myself in a familiar position, that of reacting, something that our generation has been doing for quite a while now. . . . I

find myself reacting just briefly to some of the things
that Senator Brooke said," she stated. A few gasps
were heard in the audience. The graduating students
exchanged sideways glances and checked their smiles.
For a few minutes Hillary spoke extemporaneously, re-
buking Brooke. Then she segued into her prepared remarks. "The challenge now is to practice politics as the
art of making what appears to be impossible, possible.
. . . We're not interested in social reconstruction; it's
human reconstruction," she said. Her speech wandered and wondered, its form and its abstraction striking as opposite a note to Brooke's traditional address
as possible. "Words have a funny way of trapping our
minds on the way to our tongues, but they are necessary means even in this multimedia age for attempting
to come to grasps with some of the inarticulate, maybe
even inarticulable, things that we're feeling. We are, all
of us, exploring a world that none of us understands
and attempting to create within that uncertainty. But
there are some things we feel, feelings that our prevailing, acquisitive, and competitive corporate life, including, tragically, the universities, is not the way of
life for us. We're searching for more immediate, ecstatic, and penetrating modes of living."

It was a moving, if somewhat tortuously written
speech. But few in the audience made the attempt to
follow it. The long sentences were punctuated by the
sounds of people moving and folding chairs creaking.
A murmur of whispered commentary buzzed under
her words. "Hillary had just sort of launched off on her
own," observes Acheson, one of the leaders of the
speechwriting campaign. "Some people, largely mothers, thought it was just rude and never got off that
point. And another group thought she was absolutely
right. It distracted a lot of people." But the students

loved it. "She gave it to him, no ifs ands or buts about it," recalls Schechter.

An excerpt from Hillary's speech—and her picture—made *Life* magazine. Published alongside a few others, it seemed absolutely tame.

"Traditionally, commencement exercises are the occasion for fatuous comments on the future of the graduates present," read the abridged text of revolt-minded Stephanie Mills, a senior from Mills College. "My depressing comment on that rosy future, that infinite future, is that it is a hoax. . . . Our days as a race on this planet are, at this moment, numbered, and the reason for our finite, unrosy future is that we are breeding ourselves out of existence. . . . I am terribly saddened by the fact that the most humane thing for me to do is to have no children at all."

"Realities exist but they're not real to me" was the catch phrase of another excerpt, this time from a speech by Brown University's student leader, Ira Magaziner (who, incidentally, ended up on Bill Clinton's transition team).

By the time Hillary Rodham graduated from Wellesley College, she had enjoyed triumphs and gained a notoriety far beyond even her most ambitious dreams. Her commencement speech had received national press notice. Her success on the TV quiz show *College Bowl* had brought pride to her school. She would enter Yale University with a reputation preceding her. She was well liked and, even better, respected. "I thought she'd be the first Supreme Court justice who was a graduate of Wellesley," Schechter recalls.

But outside the sheltered enclave of the progressive women's college, life wasn't always so triumphant. Hillary's conversion to McCarthy's ideals put her in direct conflict with her conservative father. When fights flared between them, the bottom line always was politics. Hillary's switch to the Democratic party was not, one might say, in a time of university takeovers, "tuning out" and "turning on," a major rebellion. But in her family it was, and the dissenting words at the dinner table sometimes cut deep.

"All of us talked about the difficulties of going back home again," reflects Kris Rogers of that time. "Our personal evolutions mirrored so much what was going on in the times, and we all went through conflicts—my dad voted for Goldwater. We were asking ourselves: how can we be children of these parents?—but then realizing that we very much were."

Outside the family, there were other problems as well. "People gave her a hard time because she wanted to be the best," Dorothy Rodham told *Paris Match*. "I think that those years were those of her greatest challenge. She was a young woman and was the equal of men. At that time that wasn't yet accepted."

"She was an unusual young woman," a classmate says. "She wasn't the same as other people in that everybody was usually more or less *of* something, and Hillary was really quite unique. She had a very strong personality. She wasn't everybody's cup of tea."

In some ways, Wellesley in Hillary's time still had one foot in the 1950s. First-year students had to be in their dorm rooms by nine o'clock most nights, and the nights they were allowed out until one were few and far between. (In later years, Jeff Shields notes, parietals were "honored in their breach.") Freshman women were assigned a "big sister," who helped them out with orientation, gave advice, kept them out of trouble, and exchanged gifts with them at Christmas. While Hillary's class was considered a swing year in terms of the changes affecting the school and the country, it did not by any means mark a radical break with past classes in terms of students' personal ambitions.

Although Wellesley was known as a place full of extremely intelligent, highly motivated, and intellectual
women, the majority of students still saw themselves
as unlikely to do anything other than marry and raise
families after college, and to use their superior Wellesley educations to be "serious adjuncts" to their husbands' professional careers, as Kris Rogers says. Although Hillary's class was the first to produce any
number of graduates aimed for law school, virtually
none of even the most ambitious of those women en-
visioned entering politics as a viable possibility for
their future lives.

The trials Hillary faced as an adolescent, as a smart,
motivated girl breaking down barriers in a man's
world, Dorothy Rodham said, made the troubles of the
1992 campaign look like a cakewalk. "The most difficult time of her life [was] when she was at Wellesley."

If Hillary Rodham did suffer as a young woman
fighting on the front lines of generational change, it
didn't show in her face. In her Wellesley senior yearbook portrait, she is a picture of free-spiritedness. She
perches on a rock by the lake, one leg dangling, ready
to kick, her body arching slightly as she laughs, her
hair straight and long. Set against the backdrop of her
classmates, a few of whom pose demurely, engage-
ment ring carefully mounted on folded hands, while
others flaunt Jackie Kennedy-esque suits and pearls,
she seems strikingly young, almost childlike. Oddly,
she looks more like she does right now than she does
in pictures taken ten years ago.

Eleanor Acheson says she's always admired the
happy strength that Hillary was able to project then.
"I've known a lot of people who are enormously
gifted, but many of them are tortured by insecurity,
have parents driving them, and there's sort of a mess
associated with it. Hillary never had any of that."

"She had a sort of quiet confidence," concludes Dana Semeraro.

Given her political inclinations and natural talent for leadership, law school was a natural choice for Hillary. She considered Harvard Law but leaned toward Yale, in part because of its emphasis on political philosophy, and partly due to an unpleasant experience she had had with a professor at Harvard.

As Hillary explained to the *Arkansas Gazette*: "I met a very distinguished, older law professor, and my friend who attended Harvard Law School said, 'Professor So-and-so, this is my friend. She's trying to decide whether to come here next year or attend our closest competitor.

"This tall, rather imposing professor, sort of like a character from *The Paper Chase*, looked down at me and said, 'Well, first of all, we don't have any close competitors. Second, we don't need any more women.' That's what made my decision. I was leaning toward Yale anyway, but that fellow's comments iced the cake."

"Hillary Rodham is by far the most outstanding young woman I have taught in the seven years I have been on the Wellesley College faculty," Alan Schechter wrote in his letter of recommendation to the Yale Law School admissions office. "I have high hopes for Hillary and for her future. She has the intellectual ability, personality, and character to make a remarkable contribution to American society."

Neither Schechter nor any other of Hillary's friends or teachers harbored any doubts that law school would be for her a training ground for political activism.

"She was going to law school not for the purpose of making money or becoming a corporate lawyer," Schechter says, "but for the purpose of using the skills and the opportunities in the legal field to influence the course of society."

Jeff Shields agrees. "She did not go to law school because she was particularly interested in being a lawyer. Yale Law in particular fit in with her general interest in governmental action."

By that time Shields himself was at Yale Law School, although, after one last Harvard–Yale game together, the pair's relationship had all but fizzled out. "The primary basis of our relationship was cerebral," he says. "It was a close dating relationship and we had a lot of fun, but it was primarily intellectual. It was one of those situations where both parties become less romantically interested in each other on a parallel track but remain friends."

Yale Law School marked the beginning of a new intellectual journey for Hillary Rodham. It also poised her for a romantic adventure. Romance and intellect would mix and meet, and the result would indeed be, as Schechter had predicted, remarkable.

2

Hillary Gets Serious

Yale Law School in the early 1970s was, as it is today, the most public service-oriented of the top law schools in the nation. The generation of law students who filled Hillary Rodham's class of 1972 had as young teenagers formed their dreams through the speeches of John F. Kennedy, and had come of age in the turbulence of the late 1960s. As a group they hoped for change, and believed that the system could make it happen. They studied Charles Reich's *The Greening of America* and discussed revolutionizing conventional notions of property. They demonstrated, they held teach-ins. In Hillary's second month on campus, they went on strike.

Many of the professors at Yale inspired her as models of the kind of professional career paths she might take toward public service. Several had even been members of John F. Kennedy's administration, including Burke Marshall, the former director of the Civil Rights Division in the Justice Department, who had been responsible for drafting much of the civil rights agenda for the federal government in the South.

At Yale Law School, Hillary's politicization progressed rapidly. For a short period of time she was on the editorial board of the now defunct *Yale Review of Law and Social Action*, an alternative legal journal that was dedicated, as its editors stated, "to the development of new forms of journalism which combine scholarship of the highest standard with reflections and recommendations based on experience and practice." The journal aimed to provide a forum for activists and community leaders as well as scholars. Its first issue featured a cover photo of national guardsmen in riot gear; its second was devoted largely to the Black Panthers.

Hillary Clinton recalls her years at Yale as a time of "trying to reconcile the reasoned, ordered world we were studying with what we saw around us." In a speech to her former classmates at a Yale Law School alumni weekend in October 1992, she said, "There was a great amount of ferment and confusion about what was and wasn't the proper role of law school education. We would have great arguments about whether we were selling out because we were getting a law degree, whether in fact we should be doing something else, not often defined clearly but certainly passionately argued. That we should somehow be 'out there,' wherever 'there' was, trying to help solve the problems that took up so much of our time in argument and discussion. . . . Those were difficult and turbulent times."

It was precisely the kind of hothouse atmosphere that she loved. The sort of contentions, complicated time in which her skills as conciliator and leader could thrive. Hillary Rodham would emerge from Yale with even greater negotiating skills and advocacy experience. She also would emerge a woman torn between love and the glories of professional life.

"And not only that, we grow the biggest watermelons in the world."

These words were to change the course of her life, though Hillary didn't know it then. She turned to look at the speaker.

"Who is that?" she asked a friend.

"That's Bill Clinton from Arkansas"—the friend shrugged—"and that's all he ever talks about."

Really? It couldn't be true. Hillary stole a glance over at the handsome, cheerful man with the voice oddly reminiscent of Elvis's. I have to find out who that is, she thought.

Bill Clinton at Yale was a long-haired, bearded Rhodes scholar who had spent enough time in graduate school already to know when to study seriously and when to put things in perspective. He was a bit older than the average law student, and bore more responsibilities. Although he had been fortunate enough to be chosen for one of Yale's few law school scholarships, the money was nowhere near enough to cover even the most meager costs of living. To meet expenses he was forced to hold as many as three part-time jobs at once. In the course of his years at Yale, he taught at a small community college, staffed for a city councilman in Hartford, and worked for a lawyer in downtown New Haven.

Like Hillary, he had clearly not come to law school to prepare for a career on Wall Street. Politics was his destiny. During his first three months of law school, he worked full-time on a political campaign, only starting to study for his classes after the November election. He then amazed his worried friends by acing all his finals.

In many ways Bill Clinton was a perfect match for Hillary: attractive, filled with high energy, committed to public service. Like Hillary, he was a highly visible, unusual figure on campus. He was the only white student who dared break with lunchroom protocol to sit regularly at the all-black students table. And, like Hillary, Bill Clinton was a classic overachiever. In high school he had been vice president of his class, and had been in both the band and Key clubs. Never mind his role as senator in Boy's Nation, through which he got to shake John F. Kennedy's hand.

"He had to be the class leader," Carolyn Staley, a high school friend of Clinton's explained to Charles Allen. "He had to be the best in the band. He had to be the best in his class—in the grade. And he wanted to be at the top. . . . He wanted to be anything that put him at the forefront."

Bill Clinton and Hillary Rodham's first close contact came during a course on political and civil liberties. It was a class not attended very often, because the professor had written the textbook and was known to be a better writer than speaker. Bill followed Hillary out of class once, on a rare day when both had been present. He trailed her closely but couldn't work up the courage to speak to her. He was shocked at himself; he'd never been shy before. Something about the woman with the thick glasses intimidated him.

"I could just look at her and tell she was interesting and deep," he later told *Vanity Fair*.

A few days later, they happened to end up within staring distance in the Yale Law School library.

The story of their first meeting has become the stuff of legend. Both Bill and Hillary told it countless times over the course of the campaign, and both say they can still picture the spot where they first spoke in the library in their mind's eye. The problem is that they remember different spots. The disparity has become a recurring source of dinnertime debate, and both have been known to recruit Yale friends as witnesses in an effort to amass evidence for each other's position.

One thing they do agree on is that on that fateful night, Bill Clinton was standing at one end of the law library, pretending to be involved in a conversation, and all the while staring at Hillary Rodham as she pantomimed studying at a table at the other end of the room.

"This guy was trying to talk me into joining the *Yale Law Review* and telling me I could clerk for the U.S. Supreme Court if I was a member of the *Yale Law Review*, which is probably true. And then I could go on to New York and make a ton of money. And I kept telling him I didn't want to do all of that. I wanted to go home to Arkansas. It didn't matter to anybody [in Arkansas] whether I was on the *Yale Law Review* or not. . . . I just didn't much want to do it," Clinton told Charles Allen. "And all this time I was talking to this guy about the *Law Review*, I was looking at Hillary at the other end of the library. And the Yale Law School library is a real long, narrow [room]. She was down at the other end, and . . . I just was staring at her. . . . She closed this book, and she walked all the way down the library . . . and she came up to me and said, 'Look, if you're going to keep staring at me, and I'm going to keep staring back, I think we should at least know each other: I'm Hillary Rodham. What's your name?' "

At which point, Bill Clinton has said, he drew a total blank.

In many ways, Bill and Hillary were perfectly suited for each other. On an early date, they held a discussion of diplomatic policy in Africa, and both came away enthralled.

They both were stars, with reputations preceding

them. Hillary had started at Yale with a certain notoriety for her multiple wins for Wellesley College on the popular TV quiz show *College Bowl*. Having had her picture in *Life* magazine hadn't hurt her reputation any either. She had already met some of the big names in Washington when she'd been invited, after receiving notice for her Wellesley speech, to a conference of young leaders sponsored by the League of Women Voters. There she'd met Peter Edelman, Robert Kennedy's former legislative assistant, and Vernon Jordan.

She had become, by the end of her first year at Yale, a bit of a campus celebrity. The image of Hillary sitting cross-legged in blue jeans on a huge lecture hall stage, keeping order as students raged at one another all around her, has stayed fresh in her classmates' minds. No one is quite sure anymore just why that meeting had been called. It might have been about the Black Panthers marching through the building, or about Cambodia or Kent State or internal problems in the law school, or myriad other things. The trials of a group of Black Panthers, including Erica Huggins and Bobby Seale, who were accused of kidnapping and murdering another Panther, were going on just then in New Haven, in a courthouse problematically located right off the Yale green, and there were nonstop demonstrations going on outside the courthouse. The trials had divided Yale Law School between the faculty, who wanted to go on with business as usual, and the students, who, unable to concentrate on contracts and torts—and failing to see their relevancy to the pressing issues of the day—talked of calling a strike. An internal sort of a trial was going on in the law school too, over the case of a member of the Black American Law Student Association whom the law school faculty wanted to sue for damaging property. Whatever the cause, there was a meeting—indeed, a mass meeting—which drew a majority of the student body in the spring of 1970. It was a bad time for New Haven and a bad time for Yale Law School. Downtown, in the streets running adjacent to the school, store owners boarded over their windows, fearful of looters and rioters, when thousands of protesters came to the city to support the Black Panthers. A fire that had recently broken out in the International Law library was thought by many to have been set in retribution for Law School Dean Louis Pollak's too reticent support of the Black Panthers. In the general atmosphere of tension and potential danger, at Yale as in embattled cities all across the nation, the students were angry and disturbed. Demonstrators had been tear-gassed on their own campus green. They were frustrated with "the system"—the government and institutions that, they felt, had no interest in justice—and they were frustrated with themselves for joining its ranks on such high levels by attending one of the nation's most prestigious schools for lawyers and politicians. Much of their anger jelled around the figures of Dean Pollak himself, who was called a reactionary, and the members of the Yale law faculty, who were seen by many students as out of touch with the concerns of the new generation of students. There were threats of violence. Passions were running high.

The law school students streamed into Room 100, a huge lecture hall, in droves, filling all the seats, cramming into the standing room at back, and spilling down the aisles on both sides. Meanwhile, Hillary Rodham led the meeting. She sat with her legs half-crossed Indian-style on the stage, one leg free and swinging in impatience. Surrounded on the podium by upperclass men, Hillary stared at each speaker intently as he or she spoke. Then, like a translator turning tortured legalese into compassionate English, she took their angry words, stripped them of jargon, disarmed

them of rhetoric, and spoke them back to them, pref-
acing, "What I think I hear you saying is this . . ."
Slowly she led the crowd into thinking about a solution
that would allow the law school to keep on functioning
but have it also address the issues that were going on
in the outside community in a constructive way.

It was an unprecedented act for a first-year student,
let alone a woman. But Hillary had the advantage of
being the person with whom everyone on campus was
still on speaking terms. She had been active during the
past weeks trying to figure out a constructive role that
the law school could play during the Black Panther
trials, and was known to both administrators and students as someone who would represent their views
fairly and, it was hoped, bring them past their current
stalemate. She'd been seen out on the green helping
coordinate marshals, trying to keep things in order so
that the demonstrators wouldn't get gassed again. She
knew how to keep calm. "She had complete self-pos-
session," her friend Carolyn Ellis recalls. "Everybody
walked out of the room. We can no longer remember
what the meeting was about—we can only remember
we were awed by her."

After the mass meeting Hillary's reputation as a
skillful conciliator stuck with her. She became the appointed spokesperson for the students with Dean Pollak, and continued to act as a bridge between them and
the administration. This meant that she was in almost
constant demand. As she had been at Wellesley, she
became a magnet for debate-addicted young women
and now men. Her cafeteria table was always filled
with friends and followers who passionately flailed
away at the issues of the day, while she sat at the center
and mediated. "We'd just stay through the afternoon,
instead of going to the library, where we should have
been," recalls Kris Rogers, who accompanied Hillary

to Yale. "And we'd sit around debating the issues and what we were going to do, what our roles were going to be."

Rogers also knew Hillary's lighter side. The two friends hung around together listening to Tammy Wynette and sharing stories. They giggled and whispered their way through antitrust class. They made frequent pilgrimages to Clark's Dairy for milkshakes, which, Hillary swore, had a high nutritional value. Nothing she ever did was wasted energy. To relax, Carolyn Ellis recounts with still audible dread, she trekked off to the Yale gym to do calisthenics—with Ellis in tow. This was long before aerobics had become commonplace and showed unusual discipline. "I was just horrified," Ellis recalls.

Little wonder that Bill Clinton was intimidated. But Hillary was undoubtedly a bit wary of him too. She was a serious, earnest person—at least in public—while he was a happy-go-lucky guy all the time. In his first year at Yale, the year they met, he shared a four-bedroom beach house in Milford, Connecticut, with three other law students, most of whom had also already done some graduate work before coming to Yale. Since they were older, had studied more, and seen more of the world, they tended not to take the law school grind quite as obsessively as many of their younger classmates.

"Bill, like many of us at that time who had come through long educational careers, wasn't as involved in the actual textbook learning as he might have been earlier in his education," explains his law school friend Alan Bersin. "He spent lots of time on political activities, and there were occasional absences—on all our parts—from the law school."

The beach house was a focal point for off-campus social life at the time when Hillary met Bill. One of his roommates, Don Pogue, was an excellent cook and made huge vats of food that the roommates devoured. On Friday nights, friends from New Haven would flock in, to eat, to listen to Carol King albums, and to discuss the issues of the day. "It was like an ongoing philosophy discussion," housemate Bill Coleman says. "We had a lot of fun."

Bill Clinton had a certain magnetism. Men and women both flocked to him, and he excluded no one—not even one highly unpopular young woman who followed him around campus, while his friends mocked her and teased him. Like his friends, he dated several women without taking any too seriously, but he wasn't considered a womanizer. There was no doubt, however, that he loved to flirt, and liked even better to be flirted with.

He projected a different kind of warmth than Hillary's, almost like the difference between the Chicago and the Arkansas sun. "You could see the differences in their regional roots," Coleman says. "Hillary was a warm enough person, but she was very precise, very well organized—and I would not describe organization as Bill Clinton's outstanding characteristic at that time. Bill was more free-floating than Hillary."

Bill was more free-floating in terms of affection as well. He had a seemingly endless well of sociability, and had hundreds of friends, among whom he barely drew distinctions of acquaintanceship or close friendship. Hillary, on the other hand, had then, as now, a small circle of very close friends, and then a great many more acquaintances.

"Hillary was intense in her likes and dislikes," Alan Bersin recalls. "She never suffered fools happily. She was direct, she could be sharp, but she also could be very warm to people she liked and trusted. She was recognized as one of the real cutting intellects of the law school when she was there, and she was very definite in her opinions."

Ultimately, it didn't matter if Bill Clinton and Hillary Rodham were similar or different; temperamentally, they were perfectly complementary. It's easy to imagine the sparks that must have flown when Hillary's intensity met Bill's joviality as they locked gazes for the first time. Bill Clinton's was a look that devoured; when he spoke to someone he had the unique ability to make him or her feel that the two of them were the only people who existed in the world at that moment. He gave people the sense that he was absorbed in them and cared deeply about what they had to say. He also knew how to draw them out so that they ended up speaking of things close to their hearts.

Hillary had that intensely attentive quality too, though what she attended to in people was somewhat different. "Hillary was a straight-shooter—there was absolutely no b.s. about her," a classmate, Harlon Dalton, who now teaches at Yale Law School, told the *Legal Times*. With Bill Clinton, "she saw right past the charm and saw the complex person underneath. I think he found that irresistible."

It may have been refreshing—and a bit scary—for Bill Clinton, who had put memories of a painful adolescence behind him in the course of becoming a world-traveled, Georgetown-educated Rhodes scholar, to come up against a woman who not only equaled him in intellect and energy, but could use her passionate mind to read and analyze him.

Certainly friends saw the potential for disaster in their union. "They were both very strong personalities," Kris Rogers says. "They were both ambitious— they both had aspirations to make a mark on the world. And what is often the case with those types of couples is that they either work wonderfully or fail miserably; there's no in-between. And so we were all kind of holding our breath, wondering if it was going to work or not. But we knew that if it did work, it was going to be a dynamite partnership."

The dynamic duo had their first taste of team action when they both became involved in a Barrister's Union prize trial. This clinical practice, in which people teamed up to prepared mock trials before a judge and jury of local New Haven people, was just the sort of high-pressure competition that both Bill and Hillary have always loved.

Hillary Rodham and Bill Clinton as a team were rationality meeting intuition, though in their case the typical male and female roles were reversed. "Law teaches a form of reasoning," Richard Stearns, an old friend of the Clintons sums up. "Hillary absorbed it; I'm not sure Bill did. Bill is a more organic thinker, he tends to absorb information from all directions and mull it through, and I'm not quite sure how his thought process works—it's more intuitive, though he often gets to the same result. Hillary's is more rational in the eighteen-century sense."

For the Barrister's Union, Bill Clinton's inchoate brilliance and Hillary's rational coherency should have added up to a stellar team. They certainly prepared hard enough. And they certainly had enough fun. Kris Rogers, who played key witness to the Rodham/Clinton legal team as they practiced for their mock trial, remembers how Hillary coached her to perfect her role as a "sultry, lying witness" whom Bill would destroy in cross-examination on the stand. "She really had the part down pat," Rogers recalls. "She was just cutting up. She could be a real ham."

The pair had a bad day, though. Hillary showed up in a bright red-orange dress that seemed to blind the judges to the finer points of her argument. Bill, however, was dazzled. "He talked about how good she was when they were working on it and when it was over," Carolyn Ellis says. "He was incredibly proud of her."

After the trial, there was no doubt in anyone's minds that Bill and Hillary were becoming a serious couple. Daring to break the tacit Yale Law School rule against student relationships, they lived together during her third year at Yale, in a typical New England Victorian-style house with a pillared porch right off campus. It was a place where people gathered to unwind in the evenings, to listen to Jefferson Airplane, the Rolling Stones, and Janis Joplin, share potluck dinners and talk the night away. They also went over to Robert Reich (now Clinton's appointee for labor secretary) and Nancy Bekavac's house on Chapel Street. As usual, they spent most of their time talking.

"Hillary felt passionately about the issues of the day, as did Bill and many of the rest of us," recalls Allan Bersin. "They were a dynamic couple, and the quality of conversation was good."

"We talked politics," Rogers says. "Not just New Haven politics, or Connecticut politics, or national politics, but global politics."

New Haven, like Wellesley, Massachusetts, didn't offer a glittering night life. The most venturesome of students hung out in the beer bars in the black part of town. Hillary and Bill hung out with friends at New Haven's pizzerias, went out for drinks, lingered in cafés and pubs, and talked, talked incessantly.

It was a time when most university students smoked pot, drank more heavily than people do today, and made the most of the pre-AIDS sexual revolution. Though we know that Bill Clinton partied hard but never figured out how to inhale, the facts are less clear about Hillary. She was not known by any means as a heavy drinker or a pothead, but, as one classmate recalls, "she's not a super-straight person. She was pretty socially relaxed, easygoing, somewhat earthy. She was not a Pat Robertson type of person who would leave the room if someone did something she didn't do. She wasn't an uptight person at all."

Before Bill Clinton, Hillary had dated a number of men at Yale. She was not a woman who ever lacked male company. "She was the kind of person who wanted a steady guy," another classmate says, "but she was not a shy violet."

Bill and Hillary had been ambivalent about a relationship almost from the start. They were both consumed by career dreams and fearful of absorption with each other. They also knew that their relationship was deep, and that frightened them. And there was always the issue of Arkansas.

"I loved being with her, but I had very ambivalent feelings about getting involved with her," Bill Clinton told *Vanity Fair*. From the time of their earliest dates, he had told her, "You know, I'm really worried about falling in love with you, because you're a great person, you could have a great life. If you wanted to run for public office, you could be elected, but I've got to go home. It's just who I am." He really didn't want to get hurt. And Hillary didn't want to be rushed into any decisions.

Dorothy Rodham was perhaps more clear-headed than either of them. She saw clearly that matters had taken a serious turn when, the day after Christmas, Bill Clinton showed up at her door. Hillary had told her simply that a "young man" she had met at Yale was coming to stay for a few days. The first encounter was, for Bill, rather harsh. He had driven the whole way from Little Rock in one stretch. That was the route that his father had taken, in the opposite direction, on the

night he had died. When he rang the Rodhams' door-
bell he was white with tiredness. He was nervous too.

Dorothy opened the door for him. She saw right
away that her days with her single daughter were
numbered.

"Hello, I'm Bill Clinton," he said, hopefully.

"That's nice," she answered.

"The introductions were pretty chilly," Dorothy
Rodham admitted to *Paris Match*. "To be honest, I sort
of wanted him to go away. I knew he had come to take
my daughter away."

Hillary was in her room on the second floor. Dorothy watched as Bill went up the stairs to find her. "It
dawned on me to ask myself what kind of character he
was," she remembered. "I knew nothing of him. But,
I don't know why, I trusted him. He stayed a whole
week. He slept in Tony's room. My husband and I
made sure he stayed in there."

After a frigid first two hours the visit went surprisingly well. Dorothy's motherly concerns were no
match for Bill's well-tested charm. On his second day
in Park Ridge, he came into the living room, where she
was reading philosophy for an extension course she
was then taking at a local college. He asked her which
thinker interested her the most. And then proceeded
to deliver a short monologue on the subject. Dorothy
was thrilled. She had long yearned for someone at
home with whom to discuss philosophy. "He was brilliant," she said, "and from that moment on, I loved
him right away."

Bill and Hillary spent the holiday week going out
with friends and taking long walks in the park. They
drove into downtown Chicago one night and went to
the theater. Bill drew the Rodham family into card
games, carefully keeping his competitiveness in polite
check. The Rodhams welcomed his efforts.

Bill and Hillary brought their mealtime volubility to Park Ridge with them. Dorothy Rodham still remembers the endless conversations. "It was always the same subjects: Arkansas! American society! They never stopped thinking. They were amazing. We could listen to them for hours on end because they spoke from their hearts, and they were really concerned with people. They had a very humanist vision of America."

Deep down, she knew that it was only a matter of time before Bill and Hillary were married. She also knew that the decision would be tough for her daughter to make. She asked Bill one day what his hopes for the future were after law school. Arkansas, he said. The answer did not thrill her.

"Okay," she said, "you'll go back to Arkansas to realize your ideals, but what about my daughter?"

The question was unanswerable and they both knew it.

Hillary, meanwhile, was taking steps to move closer to her own ideal study of law in society.

One day in the spring of 1970, while picking through the notices on the crowded Yale Law School bulletin board, Hillary saw a very small announcement that Marian Wright Edelman, a fellow Yale Law School graduate and veteran civil rights lawyer, was coming to speak on campus. She had met Edelman briefly once before, at the League of Women Voters' young leaders conference. She knew that Edelman had been the first black woman to pass the bar in Mississippi, and she had read a short article about her in *Time* magazine earlier that semester. She was eager to meet the woman whose work seemed to parallel so many of her own dreams. At the lecture, Edelman spoke about her experiences as a civil rights lawyer, and urged the students in the audience to use their Yale degree on behalf of the poor. She was preaching to the converted, as far as Hillary was concerned. After the talk she approached Edelman and asked if she could work during her summer break for the Washington Research Project, the public-interest group that Edelman had founded not long before. Edelman welcomed the chance to bring aboard an enthusiastic new recruit, but said she had no money to pay her. Hillary asked her whether, if she could figure out how to be paid, she could come to work for her.

Edelman said of course.

Hillary set her mind to finding some funds. She went to the dean's office and discovered that the law school offered something called a Law Student Civil Rights Research Council Grant, a small stipend that supported law students who were trying to work in the area of civil rights law. Her first summer out of law school, while her classmates got their initial taste of lawyerly corporate life, Hillary went to Washington.

Edelman sent her to work with Senator Walter Mondale's subcommittee, which was studying the conditions of workers in migrant labor camps. She did interviews with workers and their families, assessing the hardships their children suffered. She later studied the problems posed by segregated academies that were fighting for tax-exempt status under the Nixon Administration. She returned to New Haven afterward with her interest in children now backed by professional experience and a sense of her own potential for accomplishment.

At that point Hillary sought out faculty members with whom she could further her interests in children's legal theory and increase her knowledge of child development. She began working with Yale professors Joseph Goldstein, a psychologist, and Jay Katz, a psychiatrist, both of whom taught courses on family law. Goldstein's course on children and the law fascinated her. Katz's family law course proved a particular thrill when, for four weeks of the semester, he brought in the famous child psychoanalyst Anna Freud, a co-founder of Yale's Child Study Center, and Sigmund Freud's daughter, to help teach the class. Hillary was an avid participant in the course, a lecture that was run like a seminar. Her insights and enthusiasm stood her well.

Encouraged by her work with Goldstein, Katz, and Freud, and motivated perhaps in part by a wish to spend an extra year with Bill Clinton, who was a year behind her, Hillary applied to a law school program that allowed her to study children's rights under the law for credit at Yale's Child Study Center. There, she worked with faculty member Sally Provence on child development. And she also helped research a book, *Beyond the Best Interests of the Child*, which was published in 1973 by Freud, Goldstein, and Albert Solnit, who was then the director of the Yale Child Study Center and is now commissioner of Connecticut's Department of Mental Health. The thesis of the book was to set standards for evaluating the best interests of the child in regard to conflicts in custody placement.

Working with Anna Freud and other faculty members, Hillary participated in direct observations of children at play. She assisted the center's nursery school teachers, observed while diagnostic tests were conducted, and took part in a reading seminar on child-development literature. She applied herself to learning what she could about children's developmental goals and needs with as much rigor as she had earlier directed to the field of law. Her focus was particularly directed at normal childhood development and its variations. She impressed her instructors with her understanding of, and compassion for, the complexity and depth of children's lives.

Marian Wright Edelman remained a part of her life throughout this time. While Hillary was at the Child Study Center, her friend and mentor recommended her for a job doing legal research for the Carnegie Council on Children, which had been established by the nonprofit Carnegie Corporation in New York the year before to examine the conditions of children in America. While on the council, she wrote a number of background papers on children's legal rights and collaborated on what became then council head Kenneth Keniston's important book, *All Our Children*. She helped assemble a chapter covering children's rights to education in face of obstacles placed either by parents who refused to send their children to school or by schools that without good cause suspended or expelled problem children. The chapter also discussed children's rights to medical care, in the context both of problems posed by parents' refusing them medical care, as in the case of Christian Scientists, and of parents who needlessly subjected their children to experimental or extreme treatments like sterilization, shock treatments, or lobotomies. The work on Keniston's book placed her in somewhat of an ideological conflict with her earlier work for Freud, Goldstein, et al., for Keniston criticized *Beyond the Best Interests of the Child* as a white paper giving parents unquestioned final authority over their children.

Beyond the academy, Hillary was also gaining dramatic insights into the plight of unfortunate children.

Her understanding of the complex issues of state intervention in custody grew even deeper when she began trying to create rules for child-abuse cases with doctors at the New Haven Hospital. The issue of whether or not to remove an abused child from his or her parent was not, she saw, black and white. "For some young children, abuse may be the only attention the child got; so when you remove it, there is an extraordinary guilt: 'I must have done something *really* terrible because now they do not even *want* me,' " she explained in an interview with the author Garry Wills. The standard of "least detrimental alternative," she was learning, was hardly a fail-safe tool in practice.

Hillary also helped develop programs for children at Yale's then new Legal Services Organization. She also worked with Penn Rhodeen, a staff attorney at the New Haven Legal Assistance Association who was involved in legal battles with the state of Connecticut over the treatment of foster children.

By staying at Yale an extra year, Hillary graduated in the class of 1973 with Bill Clinton. Their lives were growing more and more intertwined—for the moment. In the summer of 1972, they had traveled together to Texas, where Bill had run George McGovern's campaign effort and Hillary had worked registering Hispanic voters for the Democratic party in San Antonio. Everything they did together now seemed to raise the issue of where they'd go next and what they'd each do. In Texas, Bill and Hillary met Betsey Wright, a powerful woman who would later become his chief of staff and campaign manager. Wright had for a few years been active in Democratic politics in her native state of Texas. She was enormously impressed with Hillary, and began to harbor the hope that she would consider running for office. But Taylor Branch, the Pulitzer prize-winning biographer of Martin Luther King, Jr., who shared an apartment in Austin with the couple and codirected the McGovern campaign in Texas, recalls that Hillary wasn't even sure if she liked politics. "Whereas his purpose was so fixed, she was so undecided about what to do," he told U.S. *News and World Report*.

Ironically, the one most important thing that Bill and

Hillary had so deeply in common—their dedication to public service—was precisely the factor that threatened to split them apart. In their last year at Yale, they did not interview with any law firms, despite their excellent grades. Hillary knew that she wanted to work for the Child Development Fund, and Bill knew he was going back home. These choices distanced them greatly from the vast majority of their classmates, whose activist impulses seemed to dry up as promises of lucrative offers grew near.

"There was a relatively small number of people who wanted to dedicate themselves to the idea of social change and therefore work outside of what was considered the establishment," Bill Coleman recalls. "There were people who did that in summer jobs, but when it came down to the short strokes, most people managed to come up with justifications to explain why, in the long run, it would make sense to go and work for a large firm. They'd say it gave you the skills you needed to go on and become an effective lawyer. It was economically in their interest, really. Everybody interviewed at the large firms except Bill—and Hillary."

Bill Clinton and Hillary Rodham had different ambitions from their peers. "Everyone was ambitious," a classmate recalls. "But I see Bill and Hillary as driven by almost a religious purpose of some sort. They had the sort of late sixties sense of *we have to make the world better*. Not 'I have to make the world better,' but 'we,' all people, acting together."

The stakes involved in Hillary's decision to pursue her career independently, despite her love for Bill, were very high. She had worked hard to get where she was, and the drag of forces weighing against her success had, at times, been very wearing psychologically.

She hadn't had an easy time being a woman at Yale
Law School.

The thirty women who entered her class with her
were considered an enormous influx, even after ten of
them dropped out. And those twenty remaining were
resented by some professors, who told them they were
taking the places of more worthy men who were off
fighting in Vietnam.

"Everybody assumed we were all accepted because
they thought the class was going to be decimated by
the draft," the classmate explains. "In fact, they just
ended up with more students. So all the time people
would come up to you and say, 'I've never seen a
woman sit still and study for longer than an hour—I'm
amazed. And then the feminist group would ask you
why you weren't more militant than you were. You
were challenged all the time—from both sides."

"Hillary was considered an unusual bird," the classmate goes on. "Lots of men at Yale Law School had
never studied with women in that class, so to see
someone like Hillary, who was so competent and so
committed, was new to them. It wasn't unusual to be
a big man on campus like Bill Clinton, but it was for a
woman to be as active and successful as Hillary was."

Bill may have been one of the only men at that time
who was able to appreciate Hillary's strengths without
being at all threatened by them. He bragged about her,
and claimed she'd shown him up at the Barrister's Union. He didn't even mind when, in a particularly tough
course on political and civil rights taught by the late
First Amendment scholar Thomas Emerson, she received a higher grade than him. For some reason, his
fierce competitiveness seemed to thrive upon hers,
rather than feed off it dangerously. Hillary appreciated
this deeply.

She was attracted to him, she told Gail Sheehy, because "he wasn't afraid of me."

After graduation in 1973, Hillary Rodham worked as a staff attorney for the Children's Defense Fund in Cambridge for a few months. Then in January 1974, she got a call from John Doar, who had been hired as special counsel on the House Judiciary Committee to head their impeachment legal staff conducting an impeachment investigation of Richard Nixon. Doar was a good friend of Burke Marshall's at Yale. He wanted five young lawyers who were willing to work hard, and who didn't think they were above "grunt" work. Marshall recommended Hillary and four or five others. "I knew the counsel very well," Marshall recalls, "and he is an exacting lawyer. So the job required basic legal skills of analysis, of factual analysis, legal analysis in an area that was quite unexplored. It required a very good lawyer, young but very good. It also required somebody who would keep her work to herself, or within the work of that group, so it required somebody with judgment and sense. Hillary had a broad scope of mind and very sound judgment."

Bill Clinton was chosen too, but he turned down the opportunity. He was preparing for a political career and an eventual run for governor in Arkansas.

The decision to work apart was a tough one for the two young lawyers, but it was necessary. Hillary had not come as far as she had just to bury herself in a Deep South backwater. Neither had Bill done so to sell out so easily on his Arkansan dream. And yet, for him at least, the match was made. Clinton's mother, Virginia, had realized the importance of Hillary in Bill's future life during a visit he had made to his hometown during a break from Yale Law School. They were sitting in the car at the airport, saying good-bye, when Bill turned to her and said, "Mother, I want you to pray for me that it's Hillary because if it isn't Hillary, it's nobody."

"He loved Hillary so much at Yale," Virginia Clinton told Charles Allen. "He was really concerned about whether she really would be happy in Arkansas or would even come. But he told her going in, 'I promised myself a long time ago, if the people of Arkansas will let me, I'll break my back to help my state.' And he said, 'That's my life. And it's the way it has to be for me.' "

Hillary began work on the House of Representatives Judiciary Committee Impeachment Inquiry Staff in mid-January 1974. She was twenty-six, experienced only as a lawyer for the Children's Legal Defense Fund; her title was counsel, lowest on the professional scale.

She was one of the few lawyers on the committee staff who had attempted to do socially concerned work after law school. Fred Altshuler was another. "The vast majority of the lawyers were New York corporate types from established firms," he says. "There were a few who were out of that mold, and Hillary and I were among them. There were not many others. We were considered the radicals. I think we were both somewhat affirmative-action choices—I was the non-corporate lawyer and from the West Coast, which was considered unusual. Politically, we were certainly of a liberal Democratic mold."

The staff was headed by special counsel John Doar, a Republican appointee who had had an illustrious career in the South during the civil rights era. The Republican minority's special counsel, Albert E. Jenner, Jr., was a Chicago attorney in his mid-sixties, a great midwestern politico and party loyalist. The staff had been put together at the height of the Watergate controversy, after the Senate Watergate hearings had been aired on television. Their job as lawyers was to sift through information that had been compiled from many sources and tie it all together so that it told a coherent story. The staff began by investigating a broad range of accusations that had been made against President Nixon to see whether or not they were worth pursuing, and then to assemble and articulate the evidence against the president. There was considerable tension between Hillary's group and the permanent staff of the House Judiciary Committee, which was then chaired by Representative Peter W. Rodino, Jr., a Democrat from New Jersey, since the lawyers on the House Judiciary Committee staff did not want the historic occasion of a lifetime taken away and handed over to a bunch of outsiders.

The staff was supposed to be nonpartisan, to present facts and not to advocate any one outcome. "We were quite careful to try to avoid people who had taken positions with respect to Mr. Nixon's future," says Joseph A. Woods, Jr., who was senior associate special counsel on the staff and is now a partner with an Oakland, California, law firm. "Our purpose was to conduct and be perceived as conducting a fair inquiry into the situation, it was to follow the trail where the trail led, and we didn't want doctrinaire people, we wanted open-minded people. That was literally a requirement. We were particularly sensitive to not wanting anybody whose background contained anything that might ultimately embarrass the staff."

John Doar, a Republican with a great power base among Democrats, set an exacting standard of judicial objectivity for his lawyers. "It was reiterated to us time and time again that our job was not to be advocates, but rather to collect information and present it," Altshuler recalls. "I was almost fired at the beginning because I made some comment that he interpreted as my taking an activist role."

To a surprising degree, the lawyers did remain true to Doar's standard. They were constantly reminded that Richard Nixon was still the president, and was to be treated, always, even in discussions among themselves, with all the respect his position normally commanded. "Even today, eighteen years later, I automatically refer to it as being the President, and not Nixon, or Richard Nixon, or anything like that. That should give you some sense of the atmosphere," says Robert Sack, who headed a task force on agency abuse by the Nixon administration. "I don't remember anybody talking as though they considered it their job or some particular pleasure to get the President."

Hillary Rodham's main assignment was establishing the legal procedures to be followed in the course of the inquiry and impeachment. It meant handling subpoenas, making sure the proper legal steps were anticipated and followed in line with the Constitution. Her work ultimately led to suggesting drafting procedures to be followed by the committee in conducting the formal presentation aspects of its work, what sort of rules of evidence would be involved, a definition of the role of Nixon chief defense attorney James St. Clair, what sort of objections would be deemed appropriate or inappropriate, and the scope of cross-examination. It meant staying in the background, following Woods's lead, and being, above all, discreet.

"It was not necessarily the glamour assignment of the moment," says Woods, her supervisor. Hillary did at one point, though, get to work with the historian C. Vann Woodward, who was retained to advise on historical parallels or lack of parallels in other presidencies. She also got to listen to the tapes.

"I was kind of locked in this soundproof room with

the big headphones on, listening to tapes," she told
the *Arkansas Gazette.* "There was one we called the tape
of tapes. It was Nixon taping himself listening to the
tapes, making up his defenses to what he heard on the
tapes. So you would hear Nixon talk and then you'd
hear very faintly the sound of a taped prior conversation with Nixon, [his top aides Bob] Haldeman, and
[John] Ehrlichman. . . . And you'd hear him say, 'What
I meant when I said that was . . .' I mean, it was sur-
real, unbelievable. At one point he asked Manuel San-
chez [his valet], 'Don't you think I meant *this* when I
said *that*?' "

While her age, relative inexperience, and pronounced liberal tendencies might have made some of
the lawyers suspicious at first, Hillary's natural discre-
tion, self-direction, and cooperativeness made her a
popular member of the office staff. According to Altshuler, "She was very scrupulous in the sense of rec-
ognizing her role was judicial and not advocacy. Despite her politics, she didn't try to shape things. It was
a real sign of character."

The fact that she'd been chosen by civil rights giant
Burke Marshall gave her added clout. She quickly came
to hold her own among the high-quality lawyers assembled on the staff. Beyond her work as a lawyer, her
personal qualities made a lasting impression. "She was
very much a team player, with absolutely no sense of
prima donna about her," recalls Robert Sack. "There
was a real sense of good fellowship about her. She was
very supportive of the people around her emotionally.
We were all kind of thrown in this thing which seemed
very important, but over which none of us seemed to
have any control. And there was a vital need for emotional support. She was one of those people who was
particularly sensitive to other people when they were
down, including me, and would come over and buck

you up, and kind of pat you on the shoulder. She was really a very supportive person."

One time Sack had a work-related dispute with a senior member of the staff and was feeling very blue about it. "It was late at night, and I got out and I was upset—it was a time when your ordinary defenses were down, we were working hard, and it was very intense—and I started to walk toward my car. I had gone about a half block when I heard a scuffling behind me, and it was Hillary and Fred Altshuler, and the two of them were running after me, just to come up and say 'everything's fine,' or 'you were right,' or something—just to come after me to be sure I was feeling all right and I didn't take it all too personally. It was an extra step which meant a tremendous amount."

It was endless work, eighteen-hour days, seven days a week. The lawyers began at eight in the morning, took a quick dinner break, and then worked until well after midnight. The Fourth of July found them feeling peculiarly dutiful in their offices. Some lawyers began to buckle under the long work hours and the pressure. Not Hillary.

"She had a tremendous amount of energy," Altshuler says. "Some people were not able to handle it well, but she seemed to rebound every day, and she was producing high-volume and very high-quality work."

She was a particular favorite of Albert Jenner, who, in the midst of the investigation, turned colors, was thrown out of the minority counsel's position, and became a senior associate special counsel. Jenner delighted in taking Hillary to the Capitol Republican club, where he spent an entire half hour once trying to get her to drink a vodka martini.

On rare evenings when dinners out were possible,

she did relax over food and wine with the other young lawyers in a few favored Greek and Italian restaurants near the Capitol. Even there, however, their conversations were hushed and circumspect. The lawyers had been sworn to strict secrecy outside their offices. Any leaking of news, any slanting of information, could have jeopardized the legitimacy of the entire undertaking. It didn't make for much uninhibited socializing. And as Washington outsiders, they were presumably easy sources to tap. But that proved untrue.

"When we first got there, everybody on the committee got a letter from one of the television news stations saying, 'We're here. If you ever have any information that's interesting, do give us a call,' and yet there was virtually no leak from our committee at all," Sack explains. "But my recollection is that as soon as you got it to members of the House or the House staff, any time anything of great interest would cross the street, it would be in some newspaper the following day. The same was true of the Senate committee. The staff could keep a secret, but once it got up to the professional politicians, it was out by the following morning."

The pressure was intense, and the uncertainty about whether or not Nixon would resign or allow the impeachment proceedings to go forward created an emotional roller coaster that played havoc with the young lawyers' nerves.

"There were various points at which the impeachment investigation seemed to fizzle, and it all seemed to be very irrelevant. It was hard," Altshuler says.

As one of three women among the forty-three lawyers on the staff, Hillary was subject to some more uncommon pressures. "Capitol Hill in general was incredibly sexist," Altshuler recalls. "The number of women was minimal, and there hadn't been much of an effort made to balance our staff with women. I

mean, the affirmative action consisted in getting someone from the West Coast, and they were proud of
themselves for that."

Once Hillary accompanied John Doar to a press conference. Sam Donaldson ran after her, saying, "How
does it feel to be the Jill Wine Volner of the impeachment committee?" (Wine Volner was the woman lawyer of the special prosecutor's office.) She stayed away
from press conferences after that.

She did not, however, suffer sexism gladly. Matter-
of-factly she corrected her fellow colleagues when they
said things she found offensive. "She was sensitive to
the issue, and without being shrill at all, would discuss
what was appropriate and why," Sack says. "She was
always enlightening me, heightening sensitivity, as we
said then."

On August 8, 1974, partly due to the committee's
work, topped off by the damning revelations of the
"smoking gun" tape, Nixon resigned. The lawyers felt
a mixed sense of relief and anticlimax. Most had left
other jobs, sometimes families in other parts of the
country, to come to Washington and play their part in
legal history.

Hillary Clinton has called her experience on the
Watergate legal team "one of the greatest personal and
professional opportunities I've ever had. . . . The staff
that was put together was so professional, experienced. I was just a fresh, young law school graduate,
and I got to work with these people, and it was such
an historic experience." She left her committee work
an even more solid liberal, more firmly committed than
ever to seeing social change and justice done through
the American legal and legislative system. Her experience on the Nixon staff had taught her that the system
could work, and that there was nothing more exhila-

rating when it did. To her, it was the crowning point of her four formative years of legal education.

"Never have I been prouder to be a lawyer and to be an American than I was during those months . . . as we struggled to define the constitutional meaning of impeachment and to carry out our obligations with the highest professional standards," she said in her speech to her alumnae class. "It was both a great relief and, I thought, a great credit to the president, when President Nixon resigned. But it was also a resounding victory for the system that I had studied and learned about [at Yale]."

Hillary Rodham was clearly destined to be a political player of some sort. But first she would have to let her relationship with Bill Clinton play itself out.

3

"I Followed My Heart"

"Suppose I'd sat down and tried to map out my life," Hillary queried the *Arkansas Gazette* three years ago. "Do you suppose I would have said I'd be married to the governor of Arkansas and practicing law in Little Rock? There is no way. I think life presents opportunities."

Hillary Rodham had expected that her work as counsel to the House Judiciary committee would continue well into the fall and winter of 1974. So when Nixon resigned in August, she was left in a quandary. Her job with the Children's Defense Fund was still open to her, and it beckoned temptingly. But Bill Clinton had put in his claims too. He'd been down in Arkansas for more than a year now, and the strain of a long-distance relationship was wearing him thin. He begged her to come down and join him. Hillary had said no once before. "It was just as if somebody had asked someone to move to the moon," Carolyn Ellis recalls.

Now she missed him terribly, and she knew that the

relationship couldn't last forever as it was. But she was on the fast track, or better—she had played a role in history, and every option was now open to her. She had interviewed with a number of top-notch Washington law firms, and their offers were very tempting. The sense of her potential power, the thrill of her potential as one of the few women lawyers at the top agencies in Washington, was exhilarating. The idea of heading down to the second poorest state in the union, a backward state with few legal services and no legal activism, seemed like shooting herself in the foot.

"It was not on her radar screen," Fred Altshuler remembers. "It was not the sort of thing that she had set out to do. Her expectations were of working at the Children's Defense Fund or doing litigation, and she was aware that this changed her horizons and her expectations, and she had to work through that."

In Arkansas the prospects really did look dim for Hillary.

"I remember Bill called me," says Brownie Ledbetter, a lobbyist for the progressive Arkansas Fairness Council and a long-term friend and friendly critic of Clinton's. "And he told me he'd met this incredible woman, and he wanted to marry her. He said, 'You know, she's got to have a real job down here, not just some make-work thing, she's a feminist and she's just wonderful. And he said, 'Do you know of something she could do, something in the line of what she does?' I said, 'What does she do?' He said, 'Children's rights.' And I said, 'Oh, gosh, Bill . . .' There certainly was a period of time when they were working out how they could do this. And I don't think there was any problem in terms of their personal relationship about her independence—he was perfectly open to that—but perhaps her feeling that she might somewhat harm his political career, which was so clearly what he was aim-

ing to do. That relationship was a lot more complex
than a lot of people say."

After the Nixon inquiry came to an end, the legal
staff disbanded as abruptly as it had been assembled.
On their last night in Washington, a group of four
friends went to dinner in a small Italian restaurant not
far from Capitol Hill. It was a bittersweet end to six
difficult months. Fred Altshuler and Hillary had
worked so continuously together that they'd grown
close, with the sort of intense familiarity that develops
in unusually high-pressure situations. They were with
two other young lawyers who had just arrived in Washington to start new government and public-interest
jobs. Hillary joked with the rest, blowing off steam after all the hard labor, but she was preoccupied. The
three others were going on to new jobs in which they
knew they'd be doing exciting, socially significant legal
work. She, on the other hand, had just about decided
to give up a chance to work on important children's
law issues and was instead heading off to an uncertain
professional future in Arkansas. She was thoughtful
and alternatively happy and sad, like a person being
pulled in two directions by an ongoing inner argument. They teased her about missing the six months'
stress, but they knew that wasn't it at all.

"You're going to Arkansas, aren't you?"

"I don't know what to do," she answered.

The next day she was en route to Little Rock.

Coming off her experience on the Nixon team, Hillary knew she was standing at a significant point in
history. Legal activism was a new and growing specialty. The first women's advocacy groups were being
set up, and her own field, children's legal theory, was
only starting to take off. Moving to Arkansas was like
taking a step back a decade, perhaps more. It would
mean starting from scratch, with no professional sup-

port network upon which to fall back. She and Bill had an ambivalent relationship almost from day one. They were wildly in love with each other, that much was clear, but their ambitions seemed utterly irreconcilable.

The debate over who was going to go where had started when they were both at Yale. While most of his law school contemporaries dreamed of clerking on the Supreme Court after graduation, Bill Clinton had always planned to go back to Arkansas. It seemed a strange ambition to his fellow high-achievers, not least of all to Hillary Rodham. Like her friends, Arkansas was a forgotten state known chiefly for its backwoods Ozark culture and its poverty. And for racism. The one thing that every civil-rights-minded Yalie knew about Arkansas was the story of how, in 1957, nine black students had attempted to enter the all-white Central High School in Little Rock. It was an attempt to test the state's commitment to desegregation, in the years following *Brown* v. *Board of Education*. Arkansas governor Orval Faubus ordered the state's National Guard to prevent the students from entering, prompting President Eisenhower to order the Army's 101st Airborne Division into Little Rock to protect the black students and see that they were allowed to enter the school. The incident made Arkansans pariahs on the national scene. The state did not seem to an up-and-coming young lawyer an ideal spot for building a career.

"Arkansas felt to all of us, except Bill, like the end of the earth!" declares Kris Rogers.

Arkansas has a population of about 2.3 million people, one-fourth the population of New York City, spread out in an area the size of New York State. In 1975, its per capita income was less than $4,510 a year, forty-ninth in the country, just after Mississippi, and $1,300 below the national average. Because of this second-to-last standing, Arkansans delight in the expression, "Thank God for Mississippi!"

Bill Clinton was the first person from Arkansas Hillary Rodham had ever met. He wasn't typical and he knew it. It was deeply important to him to bring her home, to the place that had nurtured him before he had gone off to attend Georgetown University, Oxford, and Yale. Hillary had first visited Arkansas in 1973. Bill picked her up at the airport. His home in Hot Springs was only an hour's drive away, but he had bigger plans for his intended than simply bringing her home to meet his mother. Like a self-appointed "one-man chamber of commerce," he was going to sell her on his state.

"We drove eight hours," Hillary told *Newsweek*. "He took me to all these places he thought were beautiful. We went to all the state parks. We went to all the overlooks. And then we'd stop at his favorite barbecue place. Then we'd go down the road and stop at his favorite fried-pie place. My head was reeling because I didn't know what I was going to see or what I was expecting."

To say that the sight of her future home did not enchant Hillary would be a gross understatement. But she did take the Arkansas bar exam that summer. Ellen Brantley, a chancery court judge in Little Rock who was at Wellesley with Hillary, was surprised to hear her name in roll call when she showed up to take the test herself.

"I was floored," Brantley says. "I knew she was from Chicago, and I couldn't figure out why she would be taking the bar exam in Arkansas. So sometime during the course of the test I asked her, 'What in the world are you doing here?' and she said that she had her job with the Children's Defense Fund and that she needed to be admitted to the bar of some state, that it didn't make much difference what state, and she had chosen Arkansas."

Hillary left it up to Brantley to figure out just why, out of fifty potential state bar exams, Arkansas' was the most attractive. She wasn't advertising her commitment to Bill Clinton then—perhaps not even to herself. But the symbolic gesture of laying down professional roots in his home state could not have been lost on Clinton. For the next year he asked her to come down and join him for good.

Friends fully expected her to stay in Washington. "The most likely thing I would have seen her doing over the long run was working with the Children's Defense Fund and doing something in politics," Carolyn Ellis says. "In my mind that did not mean Hillary would run for office, but that she would do something political—in the early seventies you did not think of women necessarily running for anything."

Kris Rogers disagrees. "I expected her to hold some kind of political office. I wouldn't be foolish enough to say president, but I remember we clearly thought she'd probably at least be a senator. She was an effective communicator, she was articulate, she was willing to stand up and speak out and not just shrink to the sidelines. And she had a political astuteness in terms of building bases of support. It's fair to say we did expect something political from her."

Many of her colleagues from the Nixon team and before thought she was throwing her career away. Betsey Wright, who was then trying to mobilize more women to run for office at the National Women's Education Fund, certainly thought so.

"The center of my world then was getting more women elected to office, to get women to think of themselves as candidates," she says. "Hillary was as prime a candidate as anybody. And yet I did have enough understanding of political realities to know that in the South in particular, there was a very low tolerance of two-elected official marriages. But it wasn't like that was a choice she necessarily wanted. That was just my projection, and those were my dreams."

Some friends did think otherwise.

"Hillary was very much in love with Bill, but had to reconcile what ambition she might have with marrying him," Ellis says. "She wanted to have her own independent life. She knew that he was going to do things political and go into public service, run for office. I think there was some fear on her part that she would simply be an adjunct to him. That was the traditional thing that we had seen up until that point. My response at that time was that she had no political base of her own, and she could do an awful lot down in Arkansas with her talent. I guess the only thing that surprised me is that it took her so long to go to Arkansas.

"Eventually she made an emotional decision. And she seemed so much more certain of herself once she went."

Finally it came down to a leap of faith. Caught between her head and her heart, Hillary says, "I followed my heart." Furthermore, she really wasn't sure of what she wanted to do. "I just knew I wanted to be part of changing the world" she explained to Gail Sheehy. "Bill's desire to be in public life was much more specific than my desire to do good."

"She loved him. It's as simple as that," Rogers concludes.

After Nixon's resignation, Hillary was exhausted. The eighteen-hour days had done her in. She wasn't sure what she wanted to do next, but she did know she wanted out of Washington. When she had visited

Bill at home in 1973, he had introduced her to the dean of the University of Arkansas Law School at Fayetteville, Wylie Davis. "If you ever want to teach, let me know," he had said. So she took him up on his offer. "Are you serious?" she asked over the phone.

"Well, I sure am," he answered. "I'll hire you right now."

Arkansas, she thought, would at least offer a respite from her high-pressure days and nights on the impeachment staff.

But taking it easy would have been out of character. By the third week of August, Hillary had taken up residence in Fayetteville. By the fourth week she'd learned that she was going to teach criminal law, as well as run a legal aid clinic and a project that sent students down to the prisons to work with inmates. By September she was teaching.

That same summer, Bill Clinton was making his debut in politics. Twenty-eight years old, a law professor at the University of Arkansas, he launched a bid for Congress, running against an immensely popular Republican incumbent, John Paul Hammerschmidt, in the heavily Republican third district of Arkansas. Hammerschmidt was considered unbeatable. Clinton's beginnings were inauspicious enough. His campaign operated out of a little old house on College Avenue in Fayetteville. A green AMC Gremlin took him on campaign tours around his district. Every day he drove around the district, shaking hands, making friends, collecting business cards and phone numbers, and then drove back to Fayetteville to empty his pockets full of scraps of paper onto his desk. This pile was known as a "card file." Another pile—students' ungraded papers—accumulated in the hatchback of his little car.

All that changed once Hillary Rodham appeared on

the scene. Hillary joined the campaign and rapidly became his unofficial campaign manager. Her talents as a organizer appeared instantly. She organized the office, took charge, set the team to work. Her whole family came to town to join in the effort, crossing the line to work for a Democrat for the first time. While Hugh Rodham worked the phones, Tony and Hughie took up poster duty, combing the district hanging up Clinton signs on any and every uncovered surface they saw — except trees. Hillary didn't allow them to pound nails into trees.

Although Bill Clinton did not ultimately defeat his republican opponent, he did garner 48.5 percent of the vote — the greatest number of votes any Democrat had ever before, or has ever since, drawn against the incumbent.

In the course of the campaign, Hillary got to know Arkansas — and made herself known there — very quickly. And she found, much to her surprise, that she loved it.

"I had a lot of apprehension, partly because I didn't know anybody and did not know how I'd be received," she told Charles Allen. But, she said, "the people were warm and welcoming to me. It felt very much at home. And it was a shock to me because I had never lived in the South or in a small place before. It gave me a perspective on life and helped me understand what it was like for most people.

"I loved the university. I loved the law school. I loved my colleagues," she said. "I made some of the best friends I ever had in my life. It was just a wonderful experience for me."

Fayetteville is a tree-lined college town in the Ozark Mountains near the Missouri border. Back in the years when Bill and Hillary lived there, it was filled with big Victorian houses, and had the slow-paced street life of a small town combined with the intellectual vigor of a college town. The fraternity and sorority houses on campus and nearby Razorback Stadium brimmed with life. People talked about books and ideas, and considered themselves, for Arkansas at least, quite progressive. The town spread out around the chief campus building, Old Main, a two-towered structure that dates from the turn of the century, and its hilly streets wove around the campus, with the names of college graduates engraved in the sidewalks around the university.

Once the initial shock of being known by name by virtually every person she passed on the street wore off, Hillary thrived in the small-town atmosphere. She loves to tell the story of how once, when she was phoning a student and there was no answer at home, she called information to check the number and was told: "Oh, he's not home. I saw him leave this morning," by an operator who happened to live in the same apartment complex. She thought the law school, which had no air conditioning and was as hot as a sauna, was "fun."

"I loved Fayetteville and I loved Arkansas," she told the *Arkansas Gazette*. "I didn't know why, but I just felt so much at home."

At the University of Arkansas Law School, which had relatively few female students and even fewer female faculty members, Hillary Rodham stood out from the beginning. It wasn't just her hippie clothes and northern accent. She taught criminal law and criminal procedures her first year, and benevolently terrorized her students by running her classes in the Socratic method.

"She was highly intellectual, aggressive, blunt, very articulate, and fairly tough," says Woody Bassett, a Fayetteville lawyer and former student of Hillary's. "A lot of people initially weren't sure how they felt about her because she came on kind of strong. They were a little bit intimidated by her intellect and her personality. Some of the male students were not used to being taught by a woman with that kind of intellect, and I think it took some of them a little while to get used to it. But as time went on, people warmed up to that and got comfortable."

Unlike Bill Clinton, a warm and chummy teacher who taught his classes in a conversational way and tended to grade comparatively easily, Hillary kept a professorial distance from her students. She could be friendly and engaging in private, but did not, like Clinton, spend free periods hanging out in the student lounge, talking about classwork or current events or sports. Nonetheless, female students looked to her as a role model, and sought her out during office hours for guidance and moral support.

Patty Criner, a friend of Bill Clinton's since first grade, suggested to Charles Allen that teaching was perhaps nearer to his heart than Hillary's. But, she added, "if somebody said who's the smarter lawyer, Bill or Hillary? Hillary is. But that's her profession. Bill got through law school, but Hillary helped him. They studied together and she helped him a lot because she's really a bright, bright lawyer."

Life went on for Bill and Hillary much as it had at Yale Law School. They worked long hours and were very intense about their work. They spent as much if not more time on outside projects—his campaign, her legal-service work and fledgling advocacy—as they did on university-related duties. Evenings, and on the weekends, they spent time with a growing circle of friends, which included local political figures Bill had met on the campaign plus a good number of law school faculty members. Knowing that Bill worried that Hillary would be bored and lonely in Fayetteville, his friends obliged by welcoming her as warmly as they knew how.

"He wanted her to like Arkansas, he wanted her to like Fayetteville, he was crazy about her, and he wanted to marry her," recalls Margaret Whillock, a friend who took Hillary under her wing at that time. "It was a great time in our lives. There was a lot of warmth, a lot of camaraderie. Bill loved to tell these Arkansas stories—we all did—and we used to eat a lot, sitting around in the floor of my living room, eating after ball games and talking till all hours. It was a good place to live, a good time." There were informal dinner parties, a great deal of volleyball playing, football watching, and, as always, debate. They played charades, and a facet of Bill Clinton's character, which would only get stronger in their years of marriage, became known. He was fanatically competitive at games.

"Bill would get really into it, and if he gave a clue and Hillary didn't guess it, he'd go wild and scream," Ellen Brantley recalls. "He'd just go wild, and she'd sit there and look through a magazine and laugh at him."

After a year of living in Fayetteville, Bill and Hillary decided that if she was to stay there, they should get married. The time had come for a decision from Hillary: it was Bill or bust. They had been living apart in Fayetteville, where local mores would have frowned upon premarital cohabitation, for a year now. The situation had to change one way or the other. Bill, in his best persuasive style, tried to talk her into a ring. But Hillary remained undecided. Arkansas was nice, but it wasn't Washington. Staying in the state, she now knew, would mean subordinating her own political dreams to Bill's. She wouldn't have the mobility even to move where the action was as subsequent presidential administrations took power. There would never be room for a two-elected official marriage in that state. It was hard to imagine where she'd find a constituency anyway. And what about seeing her friends? Hillary decided she had to get a feel for what she was missing. She flew to Park Ridge to see her parents, then continued on to the East Coast to visit her old college and law school friends. She traveled to Boston, to New York, to Washington.

She visited Carolyn Ellis, who was then living in New York.

"You know, you're a very rooted person, Carolyn," she said to her friend. "Even in New York, you can create a little enclave for yourself wherever you go. That's important."

"If you want," Ellis encouraged her, "you can do it in Arkansas too."

She asked other friends as well what to do. Some told her to throw in the towel and come back East. Ellis disagreed.

"I encouraged her to go back and marry him," she recalls. "I think there wasn't any hesitancy about marrying him. It was hesitancy about making her life in Arkansas, which was still very foreign for her." Ellis continues, with a small note of triumph, "And on election night in Little Rock, I met another woman who was a year ahead of us at Yale who told me she had encouraged Hillary not to go back to Arkansas. And she told me I had advised her right."

The swing through the East pretty much decided her: Hillary would return to Bill. "I didn't see anything out there that I thought was more exciting or challenging than what I had in front of me," she told *Vanity Fair*. But the sight of the marshy, brown land stretching past as her plane made its descent into Little Rock's little airport made her heart sink again.

Bill came to pick her up at Adams Field airport. Hillary was tired and wanted to go home. Instead, Bill said, he had a surprise. "You know that house you liked?" he asked.

"What house?"

While driving one day near the campus, she had mentioned in passing that she liked a cute painted-brick house with a For Sale sign on California Drive. "Bill, that's all I said," she said. "I've never been inside it."

"Well, I thought you liked it, so I bought it," he said. "So I guess we'll have to get married now."

Two months later, it was a done deed. In the battle between love and location, love won.

The house was a cottage, really, with beamed ceilings, a bay window, and a screen porch on one side. It had glazed brick and stone mortar work and was situated on a hilly lot with a nice view. When they moved in, it had an antique bed with Wal-Mart sheets that Bill had bought, and not much else.

Dorothy Rodham was rather unimpressed. "It was just a little, tiny house, only worth a handful of money. I think there were only two rooms," she told *Paris Match*.

Down in Arkansas for a pre-wedding inspection, she ran to buy the couple some household items as a wedding present. She also took Hillary to Dillard's department store to buy her wedding gown, a natural linen Victorian-style dress with lace at the elbow.

"Eight days before the wedding, I came down from Chicago to help them renovate. Everything had to be done: repainting, decorating, getting things organized. Hillary and Bill wanted to do the wedding dinner in that house. Just family. They had so many friends that they couldn't have invited everyone."

On Saturday, October 11, 1975, Hillary Rodham and Bill Clinton were married by Methodist minister Vic

Nixon in the house Clinton had bought. The wedding was a small, private ceremony, attended only by immediate family and close friends, including Bill's mother, Virginia Kelley, Hillary's parents, and her brothers, Hugh and Tony Rodham. Roger Clinton, Jr., was his brother's best man. Hillary and Bill exchanged heirloom rings, and she kept her name. Bill was twenty-nine, Hillary twenty-seven.

"It was the simplest ceremony possible, but also the most beautiful. Truly," explained Dorothy Rodham. "To see these two brilliant students loaded with diplomas which could have brought them all the luxury and money in the world there, in Arkansas, in that modest house because they had dreams of realizing their ideals. It was so moving."

Later that day, a second, larger wedding ceremony for friends was held in the home of Ann and Morris Henry, two of the bridal couple's closest Fayetteville friends. Henry was then the local Democratic party chair as well as a lawyer, and combining local friends, family, Yale, Georgetown and Wellesley friends, Park Ridge and Hot Springs friends, Fayetteville faculty and political supporters, the wedding drew nearly three hundred people, among them attorney general Jim Guy Tucker. The wedding party, which was held early on a glorious fall evening, spilled out of the Henrys' rambling house onto porches and yards and well into the family's surrounding two acres of property. The wedding cake had been baked by a local Fayetteville man with an artistic touch, and was simple and elegant—if huge—with graceful tiers, sugary white frosting, and light cream-colored sugar roses. As the child of another law school friend played background music on Ann Henry's baby grand piano, the champagne poured freely. The guests wandered from inside the house onto the wide screened porch and out into the moonlit night and back for charcuterie and sandwiches.

"It was one of those beautiful, beautiful nights," Margaret Whillock recalls.

The mood, according to Ann Henry, was ebullient. "We all loved Bill, and we had absolutely fallen in love with Hillary. We felt like we were lucky to have gotten her to come to live in Arkansas."

The poetry of Hillary's following her heart to Arkansas to roost was less resonant, however, for many of her friends. Bill's good qualities aside, they could hardly approve of Hillary's uprooting herself from the fast track for a life in the slow lane of what they considered the Deep South. Her family too had reservations—but for different reasons. Her father was less than thrilled to see his daughter mixing family blood with a Democrat.

He did come along, however, on the honeymoon to Acapulco. It was a Rodham family affair—Hugh and Tony, the parents, Hillary, and Bill Clinton along, too—the brainchild of Dorothy who, refusing to accept the argument that the couple didn't have time for a honeymoon, found cut-rate tickets and arranged the trip *3en famille*. What the trip lacked in romance, it made up in fun.

"We had a marvelous time," Hugh Rodham told *People*.

"I was disappointed when they married," Betsey Wright told *Vanity Fair*. "I had images in my mind that she could be the first woman president."

"Hillary made her trade-offs early on, and I think she steeled herself not to look back," concludes Hillary's Wellesley College roommate in *Vanity Fair*.

By 1976, Hillary Rodham was making her presence known in Fayetteville. In March, she made headlines by urging that a coalition of women and prosecuting

attorneys push for state legislation requiring that
judges rule on the admissibility of evidence of rape victims' previous sexual conduct before it was presented
to the jury. Despite her efforts, the bill died in committee. She started Fayetteville's first rape crisis center,
and made an effort to educate the local population
about sexual violence against women, issues that were
little discussed in those days.

She also caught the attention of local journalist Paul
Greenberg, a Pulitzer prize-winning columnist who
has since proven to be one of her harshest critics, when
she publicly opposed the state university's participation in the National Endowment for the Humanities,
claiming, according to Greenberg, that those who accepted the grants would obligate themselves to the
government instead of remaining intellectually free.

The Arkansas Law Association took notice when she
spoke to their house of delegates to make a plea for
start-up funds for a legal-aid program in the Fayetteville area. Addressing the all-male house of delegates,
she spoke against a very popular, articulate lawyer
who was opposed to the idea. She began with ninety
percent of the delegates against her, but after ten minutes had three-quarters of the room won over to her
side. Not just to her cause but to her. It was a double
victory, for legal aid and for Hillary, for the exposure
helped pave the way into the good graces of the legal
establishment in the state's capital.

She was also making great inroads with her legal-aid
service for indigents. In one case, when an Arkansas
community tried to close a youth commune that had
formed nearby, she took the unpopular stance of defending the commune.

"The judge *loved* the case," she told Garry Wills. "It
was the first time he ever wrote on *constitutional*
issues."

In another case, a woman jailer called her during office hours before a hearing to report that a well-known and harmless wandering "preacher lady" was about to be committed to a mental institution in another Arkansas town.

"This is just wrong," the jailer said over the phone. "This woman is not crazy—she just loves the Lord." Hillary packed her student aides into cars and drove straight to the town. The judge threatened once again that if the legal-services people released the woman from jail, it would only be a matter of time before he put her under lock and key once again.

Hillary talked to the woman, and learned she had family in California. "People need the Lord in California too," she told her. Wouldn't it be cheaper to buy a one-way plane ticket to California than to spend tax money supporting the unpopular woman in an institution in Arkansas? she asked the judge. He agreed, Wills relates, and the case, at long last, was closed.

Hillary said recently that her years with Bill in Fayetteville were some of the happiest in her life. "We had a wonderful life there," she told reporter Landon Y. Jones. "The pace of life was so much slower, so much more open to long conversations with friends and dinners that went on for hours, where you talked about everything that was going on in your life and in the world. I miss that in our lives now."

Idyllic as that time was, it is unlikely that she and Bill would ever have been happy settling into the secluded lives of university professors. Ambition beckoned—for Bill Clinton, in the form of his first statewide elected office, which he achieved in 1976, when he was elected the state's youngest attorney general at age thirty.

The new job necessitated a move to Little Rock. Hillary tried to put down roots as best as she could, but it wasn't easy. Little Rock was somewhat hostile territory to a woman with ambitious goals. "I thought maybe I'd start practicing law when I got to Little Rock," she told the *Arkansas Gazette* a few years ago, "but there were not any women in any of the major law firms. There were not many women lawyers, period." That year, Hillary taught a course as an adjunct professor at the University of Arkansas in Little Rock. Fortunately, she had met a few of the lawyers from the prestigious Rose Law Firm while she was still teaching in Fayetteville. Several of the partners had been impressed by the way she had set up the University of Arkansas's legal-aid clinic. They recruited her, and in 1977 she was hired—one of the first women in the state to join a main-line law practice.

The early years as a practicing lawyer were tough however. Other women lawyers in Little Rock continued to be few and far between, and those she met tended to specialize in the more "feminine" field of domestic relations. Hillary drove to and from work in her little Fiat, wore frumpy clothes, and generally fell short of conforming to prevailing southern standards of women's fashion. Hillary learned a partial lesson one day, though, when, having made the unfortunate choice of wearing orange pants to work, she was called in by a managing partner to meet an important client. She was mortified—and the memory stuck with her for years.

"Back in those days she was such an intellectual that she really paid very little attention to her appearance," a society writer for a local newspaper recalls. "That was not high on her list of priorities, and you'd see her around with her petticoats showing, and she just wasn't real put together. She was probably not as aware that people were noticing as she should have been. It takes you a while to catch on."

Her clipped, professional manner, agreeable by eastern standards, proved at first a handicap. In a woman, some clients read ambition as aggression, intelligence as arrogance, professionalism as unfeminine coldness. The word *pushy* came to mind. Despite the support of her colleagues, it could not have been an easy time.

There were some outside triumphs, however. In 1977, president Jimmy Carter appointed Hillary Rodham to the board of directors of the Legal Services Corporation, a Washington-based, federally financed independent corporation that provides federal funds to the nation's legal-aid bureaus. She had gotten his attention the year before when she'd skillfully organized a presidential primary battle. Now, with his help, she was edging her way back into Washington once again. That same year, Hillary was active in the founding of the nonprofit Arkansas Advocates for Children and Families, the state's first children's legal-advocacy group. The group's mandate, to help identify the problems facing poor children in the state—poverty, abuse, neglect, substance abuse, teenage pregnancy—was close to her heart, and was quite groundbreaking in a state whose rampant social problems tended then to be dismissed with pious words and head-shaking. As the group's first president, she was involved in publishing reports on school dropouts, juvenile justice, and child care, in monitoring federal assistance programs, and providing statistics on those programs to Arkansas's congressional delegation.

She also found a close ally in William R. Wilson, Jr., a highly respected Little Rock attorney with whom she began to work on criminal defense cases. Wilson had first encountered Hillary Rodham when she had made her case before the Arkansas Law Association while still teaching in Fayetteville. He had been "doubly impressed," he says, by the way, as a lawyer, she could "appeal to your mind and your heart at the same time." The association with Wilson was a good break from the Rose Law Firm for Hillary, for its corporate specialty had never been close to her heart. Working with Wilson, she tried attempted rape and personal injury cases. She also began to make inroads into Little Rock's all-male legal establishment and, with Wilson's encouragement, to make herself known as a top, tough legal counsel for potentially skeptical clients.

"I remember one of the first things I told people when I litigated with her and against her was: She tries a lawsuit like a lawyer rather than like a woman," Wilson says. "At that point in time, some female lawyers relied on their femininity, and sometimes didn't get down to the business at hand. It was a style for chauvinistic times, and Hillary didn't have it."

Hillary, according to Wilson, was an "unusually bright . . . wise, incisive" young lawyer. She was also a particularly compassionate one. When she and Wilson took on a domestic assault case that involved an obese client nicknamed Tiny, Hillary, immediately upon meeting him, asked him his real name, and proceeded to be the only person to use it throughout the entire proceedings. "It was obvious how pleased he was, just having been shown that human sensitivity," Wilson says. "She got an excellent result in his case, and he just beamed every time she was around. And I think it started out by her getting to know him, by just calling him by his real name." Hillary won the case for her client, who later reconciled with his girlfriend.

"Hillary has a remarkable ability to speak in plain language without being condescending," Wilson says. "She gets to the heart of the matter, takes a large amount of material and reduces it down to its lowest common denominator about as fast as anybody I've ever seen. And she can talk about it all in non-legal language."

Besides being a highly productive period, it was also a period of relative calm. The Clintons solidified their new friendships in Little Rock and gave free rein to their ambitions. They moved into the yuppyish suburb of Hillcrest, and took pride in their home, a small brick house on L Street at the foot of a tall, tree-topped hill. The neighborhood was filled with young professionals, antique shops, and boutiques. Hillary and Bill lived a low-key life there, seeing friends, hosting dinners, participating in the life of Little Rock's young politicians and intellectuals. They impressed their friends with the way they worked out the fine points of being a two-career couple: both shared responsibility for house chores and respected each other's time. It was their first permanent-feeling home, and they made it bear their imprint. They took a trip to Europe together, and came back fledgling collectors. Interesting art, antiques, and mementoes began appearing throughout their house—pieces that told a story and carried memories, like an odd triptych they had found in an antique shop and loved.

"You felt a lot of love there, a lot of happy memories, interesting times, just a life full of experiences collected and held there in their home," Carolyn Staley says. At Christmastime they drove up to Fayetteville and brought back a live tree, then recruited a group of their friends to help them plant it in the front lawn. For years afterward, they drove past the house to visit that tree.

Bill Clinton proved to be a widely popular attorney general, and won the Democratic nomination for governor with sixty percent of the popular vote in 1978. The gubernatorial campaign that year, his first, found Hillary campaigning at his side, while he was deluged with criticism of his liberal views on gun control, marijuana laws, capital punishment, and women's issues. Barbs were thrown at Hillary as well for the use of her own last name. That year, however, Clinton had the momentum going to overcome all criticism. In November he defeated his Republican opponent, Lynn Lowe, by nearly a two-to-one margin. That January, the Clintons moved into the Arkansas governor's mansion. Bill Clinton's Arkansan dream had come true. Now it was time for Hillary to make a place for her dreams too.

4

A First As First Lady

Bill Clinton was sworn in as governor of Arkansas on January 10, 1979, in the House chamber room of the Arkansas state Capitol. The room was packed to capacity. Smiling proudly behind her big glasses, Hillary Rodham held the Bible while her husband took the oath of office.

The inaugural ball, held at Robinson Auditorium in downtown Little Rock, was billed as a "Diamonds and Denim" evening, to which the people of Arkansas were invited to come in formal clothes or Levi's or both. Beyond its democratic call, the theme seemed designed to convey the message that the new Clinton administration would bring the state wealth and advancement without straying too far from down-home tradition. Prosperity would be, like the 4.25 carat Kahn diamond hanging around Hillary Rodham's neck, mined in Arkansas.

If the theme of the evening indeed was state pride, Hillary's inaugural costume was like a pep rally. The

$20,000 diamond in her broach had been mined at the Arkansas Crater of Diamonds State Park, the only site in the United States where diamonds can be found, and long a source of special pride for Arkansans. Her dusty rose panne velvet gown was an all-Arkansas creation by the Little Rock dress designer Connie Fails. Hillary had asked Fails to copy the basic pattern from her wedding dress, and then had asked her to embellish it with made-in-Arkansas millinery. A bit of scavenging produced some antique black lace, jet beds, and silk embroidery—all donations from dresses worn by Arkansas ladies of the nineteenth century. The beadwork on the dress, for example, had originally been worn by one Adeline Fullilove Weems, whose daughter Beatrice Weems Bulloch had preserved it. Beatrice Bulloch also gave Fails a belt, which was cut in half into an arm band, puffing the sleeves from shoulder to elbow and fitting to the wrist for an effect "something like a modified leg-o'-mutton", as a *Gazette* style writer put it.

The unfortunate analogy made clear some of the problems that the local press was having with their new first lady. It was difficult to write the run-of-the-mill "at home with" stories about Hillary, since she was so rarely at home. Even when Hillary did perform a ceremonial function in grand style—as she tried very hard to do—the contrast between who she was in daily working life and who she was in gubernatorial dress-up was so great that some wondered if her careful solicitude was real, or if there was a sort of black humor behind them.

The dress in question ended up in the Little Rock Old State House museum's collection of first ladies' inaugural gowns, even though designer Fails has since said she wished it could be buried—like a pair of old bell bottoms. Instead, the dress was presented to the museum in a formal ceremony in which Hillary served syllabub, an eggnog-like drink made with sherry—from a bowl that had once served Ulysses S. Grant. The *Gazette* writer was delighted.

With no little excitement, the Clintons moved into the Arkansas governor's mansion, a two-story Georgian house of aged, oversize red brick recycled from old state properties and cozily situated behind a circular drive with a fountain and flower beds on six and a half acres of land. The neighborhood surrounding it, Little Rock's historic Quapaw Quarter, is largely filled with southern Victorian houses. Well-restored stately homes of stone, brick, and wood, with turrets, verandas, and stained glass windows, alternate with modest two-story homes in various stages of disrepair or renovation. It is a neighborhood of young professionals, and one of the city's few racially integrated areas, although just a few blocks away from the mansion, across Main Street, are some of the city's worst slums.

The governor's mansion, which was built in the late 1940s, features such grand and quirky amenities as a two hundred-year-old chandelier originally shipped from France piece by piece, an eighteenth-century sideboard, a nineteenth-century grandfather clock, two antique Oriental rugs donated by the late Governor Winthrop Rockefeller, and a silver service originally given by the state to the officers of the battleship U.S.S. *Arkansas* and then returned after the ship was retired from active duty (and later sunk in a nuclear-weapons test). The service includes a silver punch bowl with a map of Arkansas engraved on it, highlighting the major farm products of the state. A small retinue of servants and staff came along with the mansion: cook Liza Ashley, two other house servants, and Carolyn Huber, a former Rose Law Firm secretary who took over the running of the mansion as social secretary.

Although Hillary always made sure to express the requisite excitement over the mansion's domestic wares, convincing Arkansans to look favorably on their first working first lady took some doing. The Arkansas *Democrat*, trying to help, ran an article by its "Style" editor headlined, "MS. RODHAM? JUST AN OLD-FASHIONED GIRL," in which it was explained to readers why Hillary had kept her last name, and that they could rest assured that, at heart, she was just an "old-fashioned girl." Hillary, however, threw a small monkey wrench into the welcome effort when, in response to queries about what to call her, she said: "I'm the first lady, Bill is the first man, and Zeke is the first dog."

She also told the people of Arkansas in all earnestness: "We realized that being a governor's wife could be a full-time job. But I need to maintain my interests and my commitments. I need my own identity too."

Though retaining her last name had clearly not been a decisive issue in that first gubernatorial campaign, it had nonetheless bothered some people in Arkansas. After the election, Hillary was called upon for the first time to explain her decision. She told the *Democrat*: "I had made speeches in the name of Hillary Rodham. I had taught law under that name. I was, after all, twenty-eight when I married, and I was fairly well established."

It also, she said, made her feel like a "real person."

In 1979, Bill Clinton named Hillary Rodham to head a state board. As chair of the forty-four-member state Rural Health Advisory Committee, she helped develop a program to deliver adequate health care to people in small, isolated communities. The appointment was made without fanfare, and there were no public condemnations by partisan opponents. The Clintons, it seemed, were being given a chance to do things their own way. Arkansas was smiling on them, for the time being.

One particular development brought them goodwill as well as personal joy. In late 1979 it was officially announced that Hillary Rodham was expecting a baby. Hillary glowed with happiness; Bill was thrilled. For a few years now they had been trying to have a baby, but with no luck. Soon Hillary grew beautifully huge. But she was also under a great deal of pressure, struggling to make partner and complete her duties on an agonizing child-custody case even as she suffered with queasiness and fatigue. The stress eventually caught up with her. On February 27, 1980, at 7:45 P.M., Hillary went into labor. She was three weeks early, and things didn't seem quite right. She told Bill to rush her to the hospital. Although the couple had worked together to learn the Lamaze method of delivery, they did not get to make use of it. After nearly four painful hours, a decision was made to deliver the baby by caesarean section. Bill and Hillary told each other not to fear. Soon afterward, the Baptist Medical Center staff delivered a six-pound, one and three-quarter ounce, perfectly healthy Chelsea Victoria Clinton. When Bill finally came out of the delivery room in his green scrubs, cradling his new daughter and claiming to be engaging in paternal "bonding," it was "like he'd invented fatherhood," Diane Blair, a political science professor in Fayetteville told *Vanity Fair.* Hillary Rodham made law partner later that month.

Bill Clinton had hit upon his daughter's name in London a year before she was born. "It was this glorious morning," Hillary told *Newsweek.* "We were going to brunch and we were walking through Chelsea—you know, the flowerpots were out and everything. And

Bill started singing, 'It's a Chelsea morning,' the Judy Collins song.

"[Bill] was amazed by fatherhood," she added. "He was overwhelmed by it. I've heard him say that when he saw his child, he realized it was more than his own father got to do."

Hillary made a vow with herself that she would put Chelsea above everything else in her life. Her mother had done that for her, she knew, and she would always be grateful for it. That didn't mean, of course, that she'd stay home. But she would worry about it.

"You never know in retrospect whether you did or didn't do exactly the right thing—stay-at-home mothers, gone-away mothers, all of us worry whether we should have done something differently than we did," she explained to *Newsweek*.

Hillary had been rewarded for all her hard work with a child and with partnership. Her star was on the rise. Meanwhile, Bill Clinton's seemed to have twinkled out. The 1980 gubernatorial campaign became a nasty race. Clinton had ruffled quite a few important feathers in Arkansas with his first term's valiant effort to take on the state's big industries and utilities. Now those concerns were backing his Republican opponent, Frank White. Many of his former supporters were too. They were angry about the fact that Clinton had quite substantially raised "car tags," or license plate fees, which for most people jumped from $15 to $30 in one year. They didn't care that the goal was to repair the state's poorly maintained roads, which sometimes, in extreme weather or in isolated rural areas, became so untenable that emergency vehicles could not get through. It was the idea, the *nerve*. A lot of people were tired of Clinton's nerve. He had brought in his young, "long-haired" advisers, and they'd presumed to tell the state what to do. He'd let his wife go by her maiden name—even after their baby was born! He'd been too strident, too "arrogant," too out of touch.

The final straw was a bomb dropped by President Jimmy Carter: a relocation of about 19,000 Cuban boat-lift refugees into the federal compound at Northwest Arkansas's Fort Chaffee. Although Clinton had argued hard with Carter for more federal troops and fewer refugees, the President had said his hands were tied. Arkansas, fearful of reports of Fidel Castro's having emptied his jails and mental institutions, balked at the imposition. The state was in the midst of its worst drought in recent memory: chickens were dying, cows were starving, and tolerance was running low. When the angry detained Cubans—who had never wanted to come to Godforsaken Arkansas in the first place—rioted on June 1, and about two hundred of them escaped far enough down Highway 22 to make an impending siege of Baring, Arkansas, look possible, it was as if the worst fears of doomsayers had come true.

The image of rabid Cubans running through the streets of Arkansas past the homes of "good folks" became a perfect rallying point for the campaign efforts of Clinton's opponent. Frank White let out word throughout Arkansas that Bill Clinton had basically gone to Cuba, picked all the most violent and depraved criminals out of Castro's jails, and invited them to their state out of the perverse kindness of his heart. Shamelessly playing to voter racism, White aired a commercial showing the detainees rioting and criticizing Clinton for not standing up to the president.

Bill Clinton first saw the commercial in the governor's mansion in late October, surrounded by old friends from Hot Springs and Fayetteville and, of course, Hillary. The images were grainy and flickering, like war footage: Cubans running down an Arkansas main street, Cubans holding sit-down strikes inside the federal fort. After he watched the ad, Clinton turned to the others in disbelief.

"Do people really believe this stuff?" he asked.

"Sure they do," someone said. Heads nodded.

"See!" said Hillary, jumping up from her seat. "People believe what they see and hear, Bill. You can't just sit there and take it."

Hillary was doing what she could then to campaign, but, overwhelmed by work and busy with baby Chelsea, she had less time to devote to canvassing the state than she had had before. She'd become an issue for Bill Clinton, anyway. Her name, in particular. Letters had been pouring into the governor's mansion asking, "Doesn't your wife love you?" and "What's wrong with your marriage?" Eight percent of the voting population, it seemed, swore they would vote out Bill Clinton on the single issue of Hillary's keeping her last name.

Clinton's supporters were shocked. There were women all over the country by then who were keeping their own last names when they ran for political office. The problem was, they realized, that Hillary was a candidate's *wife*. That put her in a different category altogether.

No one was more taken aback by the reaction to Hillary than Brownie Ledbetter. "It became very clear to me then that it was all about the idea that in every marital relationship one person has to dominate or has to be the boss, that this is quite an expectation that people have, and so people assumed that if Hillary kept her own name, she must have been the boss, and therefore Bill was weaker, or not manly enough or something."

Much that has been written and said about Bill and Hillary Clinton since that time confirms that Ledbetter was probably right. John Robert Starr, for one, who was then the managing editor of the conservative *Arkansas Democrat* and is now a columnist for the *Democrat-Gazette*, played a definitive role in painting Bill Clinton as a spineless opportunist whose "backbone" was Hillary. Although Starr, who is credited with creating the epithet "Slick Willie," has always professed great admiration for Hillary, his strident attacks have generally been credited for bringing the quick end to the first Clinton administration.

Everything was going wrong. Bill Clinton was stopped on a highway going eighty miles per hour, trying to make it to a YMCA library dedication in the midst of a statewide safe highway campaign, and people were enraged. He joked that he and Hillary should name their first child Hot Rodham. No one laughed. It was a sore point. Hillary's name was just the tip of the iceberg, but it was a very pointed, and ship-sinking, tip.

In November, Frank White won the election by a margin of 32,000 votes. He called it a "victory for the Lord."

Clinton, faced with his loss, wept openly. Election night he withdrew into himself, leaving Hillary to deal with reporters and well-wishers and to extend gracious words to the incoming Whites.

For his farewell speech, Clinton appeared before a joint session of the legislature in a crowded House chamber. Hillary was at his side, holding ten-month-old Chelsea.

"I'll take life a day at a time," he told reporters. "I can't really afford that, but that's what I plan to do." He said he would look for a new office. When asked if he would practice law, he said with little enthusiasm, "I don't know. Maybe."

A pall of gloom settled over the governor's mansion as Christmas approached. Clinton was inconsolable;

friends struck attitudes of mourning as well. Hillary didn't take well to the passivist mood. Carolyn Staley remembers one occasion, at a mansion Christmas party, when Hillary's frustration surfaced, focusing itself briefly on the fact that she felt Staley, playing the piano, was choosing too morose a selection of tunes.

"I didn't realize I was playing quietly and sort of softly—not funeral home music, but I wasn't playing upbeat "Frosty the Snowman" and "Rudolph the Red-Nosed Reindeer," she explained to Charles Allen. "I was probably playing "Silent Night" and quieter things. And Hillary came over and said, 'Come on, Carolyn, pep it up. Pep it up. We've got to keep our happy face on.'"

Staley took the advice to heart. A few nights later she was at the mansion, once again playing the piano. Bill was sitting morosely in the living room. As he stared off into space, a group of carolers showed up outside his window, singing "O Come, All Ye Faithful" in particularly forceful voices. Bill and Hillary opened the door—and a group of his classmates from Hot Springs High School walked in. Staley had arranged it all.

"He sat down in one of those big wing chairs in the living room, and tears just streamed down his face," she recalled. "He couldn't believe that his friends loved him that much. That was a kind of watershed. After that he kept his chin up."

Bill Clinton took a position with one of Little Rock's most prestigious law firms, Wright, Lindsey and Jennings, and the family moved into a four-bedroom house in Hillcrest, a district where, Clinton knew, he had received 61 percent of the vote. It was a charming turn-of-the-century house, yellow with white trim, and an L-shaped porch, just around the corner from the stately stone mansions of Hill Road. It had beautiful hardwood floors and a library with floor-to-ceiling bookcases. The house should have offered some consolation to the troubled Clinton household, but there was more consolation needed than built-in bookshelves could accomplish. Hillary's career was then climbing to greater and greater heights, while Bill perceived himself, now a practicing lawyer, as sinking lower and lower. Hillary's law partner, Herb Rule, told Gail Sheehy that he believes that this became a major cause of difficulties between them.

It was a troubled time. A period of soul-searching, some might even say self-indulgence. For the next six months, friends say, Bill wasn't himself. He seemed aimless, depressed. For once he actually withdrew from people, preferring seclusion and introspection. It was as though he had been personally betrayed by every citizen who had cast a vote against him.

"It was just like he had been dislocated," says Carolyn Staley. "And that Frank White didn't win on real issues of what his vision was for people's lives, but rather on negatives like the Cubans in Arkansas, really hurt him. There was no tolerance, no compassion in that whole campaign. I think it just killed Bill that people had bought into that. He was truly unhappy, truly depressed, down. He had been split from his love, from the thing that gave him a reason to get up every morning, and practicing law just wasn't doing it for him."

Bill spent the second half of 1981 traveling around the state apologizing. "We'd go out and there'd be these confessionals in the supermarket aisles," Hillary told the *Washington Post*. "People would come up to Bill and say they voted against him but they were sorry he lost, and he'd say he understood and he was sorry for not listening to them better."

"I viewed it more as a masochistic exercise than a

depression," Betsey Wright says. "It was just this passing no one without asking them to critique him. It was from the moment he was up in the morning until the moment he went to bed at night."

Hillary, Wright says, was somewhat disturbed by Clinton's excessive self-flagellation, but apart from a few offhand comments, she kept her peace. "It was her respect for what he chooses to do. They don't inject themselves in each other's behaviors. Her tolerance for some of his behavior just amazes me."

Bill Clinton sought absolution—and comfort—from anyone who would offer it. Many people have suggested that his infidelities started at this point. Or at least that a certain looseness in his behavior set in. "Bill was always very careless, out of an unbelievable naivete," Wright told *Vanity Fair*. "He had a defective shit detector about personal relationships sometimes. He just thinks everyone is wonderful. He is also careless about appearances." Observers of Bill at this time agree that he did become, above all, very careless in his comportment.

It was axiomatic that the rumor mill would begin. News spread among reporters and gossips that Clinton was seeing another woman. In interviews in the 1992 campaign, Clinton did admit that the "trouble" he brought to his marriage began during this disaffected period. But he has never ventured to elaborate further. Nor has Hillary Clinton.

Carolyn Staley says, "I cannot think of anything I witnessed in those two years that said to me: problem marriage. It wasn't nonstop passion or anything, but I don't remember any uncivil times."

Betsey Wright, however, has frequently spoken of the "bimbos" and "groupies" who hung around Bill Clinton during those years. "They were on the streets, sidewalks, in choirs, singing at his church," she says.

"They were in the walls here. And nationwide! We'd go to a National Governors Association meeting and there'd be women licking his feet. There were always so many women who were throwing themselves at him. And he was naive about that. They'd want to take photos, and he'd stand there with his arm around them and not understand that it was naive. They'd go, 'Governor Clinton, I want to meet you,' and then the batting of the eyes and the silly gaze and the brushing of the shoulders would begin. When Chelsea and Hillary would both go and do something together at night, or when they were both out of town, his idea of a really exciting thing to do was go to the movies by himself. Well, we had rumors all over the place before the movies were out about how he was really there for some secret rendezvous or something sad like that. His attitude was: I don't care. I'm not gonna let people rob me of going to the movies by myself if I want to just because they want to make up stupid things."

"I think Hillary knew those women weren't important," she says.

Of course, the bimbo factor was nothing new. When Bill had been a teenager in Hot Springs, girls would find a thousand reasons to visit his next door neighbor, Carolyn Yeldell, just so they could look through the picture window at him. In graduate school, as a charismatic, bearded anti-war organizer, he was often surrounded by female groupies. Betsey Wright first encountered them in 1972 when Clinton ran George McGovern's campaign in Texas. And she saw them linger long afterward.

Perhaps, wittingly or not, Bill Clinton invited them.

Bill Clinton, as the step child of an alcoholic father, came into adulthood with a legacy of family dysfunction that he had almost no choice but to re-enact, to a certain degree, with Hillary. It is almost axiomatic that adult children of alcoholics will seek affirmation and approval everywhere they can find it. They lack the inner mechanism that allows them to naturally feel good about themselves, and are cruelly harsh in judging themselves. That inner cruelty, at times of failure or personal difficulty, makes the need for external positive reinforcement and approval all the stronger. If Bill Clinton engaged in a terrible period of self-blame after his 1982 defeat, it is more than likely that Hillary Clinton, as his other half, his closest friend, the person who knew him better than anyone else on earth, came to be too much of a mirror for him, her very presence reflecting back to him all the negative things he thought about himself. She knew him too well: his warts and weaknesses alike. She too was disappointed, critical of his first term in office, if not personally of him. It is altogether understandable that, under conditions that would have been so painful to him, he went beyond his marriage to seek the feeling of unconditional love and approval he so needed—the kind of love that, for people with poor self-esteem, a spouse often cannot provide.

The 1980 election brought other bad news—this time for Hillary. Ronald Reagan's election in a Republican landslide foreboded the virtual evisceration of Jimmy Carter's Legal Services Corporation. Although Hillary fought hard to preserve it, and had the deans of all the most prestigious law schools in the country lobbying Congress behind her, the Great Communicator was on a service-slashing tear. Thanks largely to the lobbyists' efforts, Reagan cut the corporation's budget by thirty percent, but stopped short of destroying it. He did, however, see to it that Hillary Rodham, among Jimmy Carter's other appointees, was unseated from the board.

Tempers in the Clinton household were flaring. Carolyn Staley spurred an odd run-in with the Clintons when she visited their house on Midland Avenue to express concern over reports she had read in the newspaper about Bill's record on commuting sentences. In an effort to ease the prison population, Bill had asked the state parole board to recommend to him which prisoners had committed nonviolent offenses and had followed their recommendations in commuting some prisoners' sentences. The newspapers had reported, however, that he was responsible for commuting sentences of the state's most violent criminals.

"I went in and said, 'I'm sorry that that happened,' and Bill said, 'It's not true,' " Staley says. "And I said, 'It's not true? I mean what's in the paper isn't true?' He said, 'No, it didn't happen. It's absolutely not true.' And I said, 'Well, I guess I just made a wrong assumption. It's reported in the paper and I assumed it was true.'

"And Hillary spun around and said, 'See, Bill!' She just screamed, 'See, Bill! People do believe what they read in the paper! Unless you come out and correct it, then people believe it's true, or if it wasn't you would've fixed it.'

"Her frustration was that he had given the benefit of the doubt to the reader and thought, 'Oh, they're smart enough to know,' or 'People have a memory and they know I didn't do that.' "

It was a concept he had to get used to if he ever hoped to fight political foes effectively, Hillary told him. This theme recurred between them again and again. But facing opponents staunchly, standing on principle, defending himself on views that were possibly unpopular, wasn't Bill's strong point. It was hers.

"When he first went in in 1979," Hillary told Charles Allen, "he was so excited about all of the challenges that the state posed . . . that he tried to do more than he had the support and understanding of the people to do. He didn't really lay the groundwork. He didn't give the kind of impression that he needed to give that he was really fulfilling an agenda that everybody held as opposed to imposing something on people. So they rebelled and defeated him."

In April 1981, in the midst of his prolonged funk, Hillary talked him into his first act of a defiant come-back. Local journalists were preparing to produce their yearly lampoon show, "The Farkleberry Follies," which usually featured a well-known person as a "mystery guest," delivering a funny monologue and then revealing his identity at the end of the show. That year the show was titled "Cubans and Car Tags." Clin-ton was asked to appear and, not surprisingly, said no. Go ahead, Hillary urged him. Make them laugh. Make them laugh, and you'll see they love you again.

So Clinton appeared in a skit where a bunch of bum-bling Cuban hijackers attempt to take over a small commuter airplane. He wore a leather pilot's helmet covering his face. At the end he whipped off the hel-met and delivered a hilarious speech, in which he poked fun at himself, and at Frank White, who was seated before him, front and center. The crowd loved it.

"You could see the change occurring in Clinton. You could see his face light up," Leroy Donald, business editor of the *Arkansas Gazette* and producer of the show, told Clinton biographers Charles Allen and Por-tis. Bill Clinton's star was on the rise once again, as he declared his candidacy for 1982, and Hillary was help-ing shine the way.

Hillary had her own personal difficulties to over-come, however. Campaigning on behalf of her hus-band again as Hillary Rodham, she received somewhat chilly applause when facing audiences around the

state. Now that voters had found once again a traditional, more palatable first lady in Gay White, who, as
her husband liked to brag, was a "full-time first lady"
and had hardly ever worked outside the home, they
gave full vent to their feelings of antipathy toward Hillary. The hostility from many quarters was palpable—
and cruel. When the Rose Law Firm moved to its present downtown location, in a renovated old YWCA
building, and held an open house to show off its new
elegant offices (swimming pool in the basement not included), Hillary was rudely rebuked by a client when
she stepped forward to welcome him to the reception.
"Hi, I'm Hillary Rodham." As she stuck out her hand,
the man began forcefully poking her on the shoulder
where her name tag was, saying loudly: "That's not
your name! That's *not* your name!"

The Clintons both took leave of their law firms in
1982 to devote themselves to full-time campaigning. At
a press conference that February, announcing the official campaign kickoff, Hillary also let drop the unex-
pected news that, while she would continue to practice
law as Hillary Rodham, she would campaign and intro-
duce herself "in non-professional capacities" as Mrs.
Bill Clinton. (Later in 1982, when she interrupted her
leave to argue one case on appeal for her firm, she did
indeed use her maiden name.)

When reporters, understandably intrigued,
pounced on Hillary with questions about the name
change, she bristled. Cradling two-year-old Chelsea in
her arms, she said, "I don't have to change my name;
I've been Mrs. Bill Clinton since the day we were married." As reporters pressed her further, she admitted
that she had not legally changed her name and that
she was still registered to vote as Hillary Rodham.

As much as she tried to disown it, the name change
was news. It received national attention—exaggera-

tions and distortions included. "Hillary Rodham," the *Washington Post* reported, under a headline reading "CHANGING ALL THOSE CHANGES," "will not only give up her law practice to campaign full-time, she also will stop using her maiden name and henceforth be known as Mrs. Bill Clinton."

She was forced to go on the record discussing it. She told a *Democrat* reporter that she had kept her maiden name when she married because it was "important to me that I be judged on my merits and that Bill be judged on his merits," but added that she had been "not at all prepared about the concern people expressed about this decision which we had made personally."

Her name had "interfered with people's perceptions of the kind of job Bill did," and, she said, "I did not want to have made a decision which would impact adversely on what he had chosen to be his life's work. After thinking about it a lot and seeking a lot of guidance, I became Hillary Rodham Clinton."

"It became a kind of growing concern among his supporters, who came to see me in droves, or called me on the phone and related story after story, and said, 'We really wish you would think about this,' " she explained to the *Washington Post*.

Bill, she said, never asked her to change her name.

"I joked one time that probably the only man in Arkansas who didn't ask me to change my name was my husband—who said, 'This is your decision and you do exactly what you want.' And so I did," she told the *Post*. "I just decided that it was not an issue that was that big to me when it came right down to it."

Although Hillary *Clinton* disavowed any great pain in giving up her maiden name, many of her friends felt otherwise.

"She was very proud when they went into office,

and he was very proud that she had kept her name," Carolyn Ellis recalls. "She wanted so badly not to lose her independence."

"She had made a deliberate decision when they got married to keep her name," Kris Rogers says. "That was very important to her. She'd already established something of an identity for herself professionally with that name, and that was a tough one. I think it felt like giving up part of herself."

"I teared up. I had a lump in my throat," admits Betsey Wright.

"You have to wonder what her options were," asks Brownie Ledbetter. "Her options appear to me to be either to have changed her name or to have left Bill. Or to have in some way endangered, or at least be accused of destroying, his career—as she regularly was. There were people who called up and said that to her, called up and said that to Bill. We live in the kind of culture where she really only had two choices. Pretty stinking choices.

"The horrible thing," Ledbetter continues, "was that once she did change her name, many of the people who were incredibly critical immediately flipped over and were so overwhelmingly positive about her, and many kept saying that she would be a better governor than Bill. It was the most frustrating thing."

It was true. After Hillary's name change, one local paper was suddenly proclaiming: "Biggest supporter is asset to Clinton," and was charitably describing her as "an Illinois native, perhaps a little brisker, a little more outspoken than the traditional southern governor's lady. . . . The name change indicates that she's working at softening her image a bit . . . and succeeding, apparently," the newspaper said. "She has become a good handshaking campaigner in the traditional Arkansas style."

Hillary began to see local crowds warming to her. The fact was, her speeches were so strong, so passionate, that it was impossible not to be impressed by her. Local journalists and political pundits started to take notice. There were calls for more, not less, of Hillary in the 1982 campaign.

The differences between her and Bill's styles became apparent, and many judged they liked her way of addressing issues better. Word was that, though she was as articulate and persuasive a speaker as Bill Clinton, she cut to the chase more quickly. People felt they could tell where she was coming from, and what she was leading them to. They trusted her. Ironically, they started to like her.

"People have to understand what Arkansas is like," Brownie Ledbetter explains. "Relationships are more important here than ideology. And relationships are more important than what party somebody's in. Because it's a small state, and because public officials are very accessible, you get to know people personally and you walk through some of those things. And that's been the way with Hillary. As people got to know her, *once she changed her name* and was willing to knuckle under, and all the macho folks were finally satisfied, then people were far more accepting, and I think most women, even feminists, understood that situation and what she'd been through."

Even though, with Chelsea just a toddler, her time was limited, Hillary maintained a back-breaking speech-making campaign schedule. In a few months' time, she won her husband more goodwill than a whole bevy of political aides could ever have hoped to achieve. Throughout everything, she sat in on all the strategy sessions for the new gubernatorial race. She plugged Bill Clinton's programs in her speeches and explained them clearly. She repackaged him. When

LEFT: Hillary Rodham, the "Goldwater Girl," in her 1965 Maine Township High School South yearbook picture. (Peter Frahm)

BELOW: Seventeen-year-old Hillary Rodham, front and center in this picture of National Merit Scholarship finalists, was voted "most likely to succeed," a high school classmate recalls. Hillary Rodham's childhood home at 235 North Wisner in Park Ridge, Illinois. (Peter Frahm)

LEFT: Wellesley College Government Association president Hillary Rodham made *Life* magazine with her commencement speech calling for a "more immediate, ecstatic, and penetrating mode of living." (Lee Balterman/*Life* magazine)

BELOW: An "adoring look" worthy of Nancy Reagan. Hillary Rodham, with the infamous "frizzy" hair and thick glasses, holds the bible as her husband is sworn in as Governor of Arkansas. (*Arkansas Democrat-Gazette*)

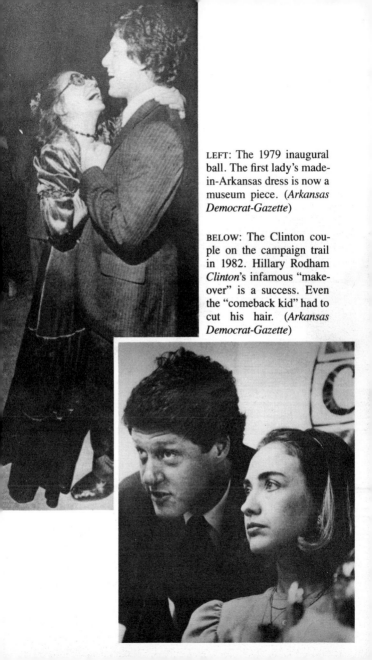

LEFT: The 1979 inaugural ball. The first lady's made-in-Arkansas dress is now a museum piece. (*Arkansas Democrat-Gazette*)

BELOW: The Clinton couple on the campaign trail in 1982. Hillary Rodham *Clinton*'s infamous "makeover" is a success. Even the "comeback kid" had to cut his hair. (*Arkansas Democrat-Gazette*)

The triumphant return to the governor's mansion in 1983. "Innocent . . . yet sophisticated." Second time around, the chastened first lady's inaugural gown used "a pleasing set of feminine contradictions to state its case," the *Arkansas Democrat* said. (*Arkansas Democrat-Gazette*)

A mother-daughter portrait with four-year-old Chelsea, named for a Judy Collins recording. (*Arkansas Democrat-Gazette*)

Hillary Clinton, in a rare show of emotion, wiped a tear from her eye as her husband announced he would not run for president in 1988. (*Arkansas Democrat-Gazette*)

The nation met Hillary Clinton—headband-clad—as she stood by her man on "60 Minutes." (AP/Wide World Photos)

Teamwork between campaign stops. (AP/Wide World Photos)

A campaign stop in Park Ridge last year found Hillary Rodham Clinton still centerstage at Maine South High. (AP/Wide World Photos)

Women of Steel, sweetly smiling: soul sisters Hillary Clinton and Tipper Gore. (AP/Wide World Photos)

The postconvention Hillary shows she's no foe of family values. (AP/Wide World Photos)

Talking points or sweet nothings? Photographers said the Clintons upped the private exchanges once they saw they made great photo ops. (AP/Wide World Photos)

"This is my choice. This is how I define my personhood—Bill and Chelsea," Hillary told *Glamour.* (Cynthia Johnson/*Time* magazine)

necessary, she played "bad cop" to complement his often too-accepting manner with campaign staffers. Her role would prove a prototype for her work on the national stage a decade later.

"When she saw a problem with the campaign structure, or when she saw people weren't producing, or when she saw things weren't going as well as they should be, she was the one who always brought it to Bill's attention, and always made sure he tried to do something about it to correct it," says Woody Bassett, who was active in the campaign.

"She had the toughness to complement Bill Clinton," Ledbetter says. "He doesn't like to tell anybody no, and she knows how to do that."

Hillary had, of course, by now changed more than her name. It was also discovered, at the February press conference, that her formerly wild hair had been cut straight, curled under primly, and lightened. And she finally found some contact lenses that worked for her, and she started wearing them.

Carolyn Ellis was apprehensive about the change. "She loved her glasses, she loved different color lenses—lenses that changed color on the outside," she explains. "This was her one fashion thing—new kinds of glasses."

Bill had made some changes as well. He cut his hair so that his ears now showed in photographs, a point of character considered important to Arkansas voters. And he changed the look of his staff, exchanging his bearded young aides for clean-shaven, middle-aged men.

The 1982 gubernatorial race bore some eerie similarities to the 1992 presidential campaign. Hillary Rodham *Clinton* was a hot political issue. Frank White, running for reelection, made every effort through innuendoes to run her against his stay-at-home wife.

The man who had won his 1980 election on racially charged images of rioting Cubans now told the state's Republican Convention in September that "you can't wash the spots off a leopard. It's still Hillary Rodham and Bill Clinton."

Presenting himself as a defender of traditional family values, from an older and more wholesome generation, he made every effort to suggest that Clinton's character was weak and tended toward liberalism. Clinton was moved to retort that his cosmetic changes had been made to better present his true face to the public and stated for the record that he had not cut his hair—yet another bête noire of his later candidacy—but started combing it back over his ears at his wife's request. He continued to assert that Hillary Rodham Clinton had always used his last name socially. In fact, on a 1977 listing of guests for a White House dinner, the attorney general and his wife had been listed as Bill Clinton and Hillary Rodham.

Hillary and Bill Clinton learned a number of lessons that campaign year. Hillary, in particular, received an education in southern politics. You can't, she found, ever trust a smiling face.

"A year or so before she made the decision, she would tell me about the positive feedback that she was getting from Arkansas women about keeping her name, she would tell me about the older women that would come up and say, we're so glad you kept your name; we wish we could have done that," Carolyn Ellis remembers.

"She took us at face value," Brownie Ledbetter says. "There were a lot of cagey old guys who fooled her. I remember her telling me a couple of things, like about how some of the ministers she had visited with understood about the Equal Rights Amendment, and I knew it wasn't true. I knew that they would never have said to her, 'I don't agree with you.' That's probably the toughest thing she had to face. We're always nice, regardless of what we think. The hostility was hard to take because people would not show it."

5

"Happy Days Are Here Again" — The Clinton Decade

By election day 1982, Arkansas was ready to hand the governorship back to Bill Clinton. The prodigal son had been chastened and could now be welcomed back home. Many voters had simply wanted to scold the young upstart in 1980. They hadn't expected him to lose. They had kicked themselves the next January, when the new right-wing Republican regime had taken office, and they'd waited eagerly for the chance to get back their state.

"There were so many people who regretted the day after that they'd made the wrong decision," Ann Henderson, an old friend of Clinton's and a campaign staffer, says. "Back in 1980 there were a lot of good Democrats who just got irritated and decided they'd teach him a lesson. One vote less wouldn't make any difference. They woke up the next morning and were absolutely shocked."

The 1982 campaign effort, an uphill battle, had been

greatly aided by the regrets many of the people of Arkansas felt then toward Clinton.

"There was a great deal of collective guilt across the state, and the zeal with which people threw themselves into the 1982 comeback was not like anything I'll ever be around again in life," says Betsey Wright.

The return to office was a triumph. The Clintons rushed their possessions back into the governor's mansion, and staked out their former home with an avidity verging on vengeance. Hillary Rodham Clinton made a ripple-free return to first ladydom. In her two years out of the mansion she'd had time to study the flawless performance of Gay White so well that her public appearances were now picture-perfect in their graciousness. This time around, though she and Connie Fails were becoming close friends, she chose a dress by a New York designer. The *Arkansas Democrat* went into paroxysms of joy at the sight of it hailing the dress as a "feminine creation . . . which relies on a pleasing set of feminine contradictions to state its case . . . innocent . . . yet sophisticated . . . soft and wispy." It was a floor-length gown of chantilly lace in an overdress ("pure innocence,") with a satin underdress "in that intriguing gray called taupe." Hillary wore with it the Kahn Canary diamond, set this time as a solitaire in a simple ring setting.

A record crowd turned out for the inaugural ball, which was held at the State House Convention Center, while an overflow of nine hundred people shuttled over into the grand ballroom of the new Excelsior Hotel. Betty Fowler's Orchestra, performing that evening, played "Happy Days Are Here Again" as the Clintons entered the Governor's Exhibition Hall. After Clinton delivered a short speech welcoming his supporters to his "nice little intimate party for a few friends," he and

Hillary danced to "You'll Never Know." It was like the
formal wedding they'd never had. Virginia Kelley and
her husband were there, as well as Roger, and all the
Rodhams except Hillary's father, who earlier in the day
had been rushed to University Hospital with chest
pains.

Hillary's transformation into perfect first lady was so
complete that old friends found her nearly unrecognizable. Kris Rogers first saw her again, after a six-year
hiatus, when Hillary came out to her new home state
of Oregon to speak to a teacher's group.

She was shocked at the changes in her friend. "We
went and picked her up at the airport, and she had this
southern accent," Rogers remembers. "I really did a
double-take; I wondered if this was the same woman I
knew, because she had acculturated so quickly. I was
really taken aback, wondering if this was a surrogate
or the real person. But then that's Hillary; she had
made up her mind to do that and had to go all the way.
She sank herself into it heart and soul."

The astuteness of Hillary's style overhaul became
clear when, in 1983, Bill Clinton appointed her to head
his new Arkansas Education Standards Committee.
Although aides warned him the appointment would
bring charges of nepotism and possible scandal, Hillary by then had become so acceptable that no objec-
tion was raised.

"We have talked about this subject more than any
other issue," he said, announcing her appointment at
a news conference. "This will guarantee I'll have someone closer to me than anyone else [as chairman]."

At the time the Education Standards Committee was
formed, students in Arkansas scored far below the national average in standardized reading and math tests.
A new report, "Nation at Risk," had just come out
from the National Commission on Excellence in Edu-

cation, and had warned of a "rising tide of mediocrity" in the nation's schools. Clearly, there were lessons to be learned in Arkansas. None of the state's 371 districts was requiring students to take all the subjects that the commission said their high school education should cover. Hillary said her committee would place its study of Arkansas schools in the context of the national report. With that framework provided, she was ready to begin.

The first problem Hillary Clinton knew she had to tackle was attitude. Students in Arkansas suffered from a terrible sense of inferiority—the "Thank God for Mississippi" syndrome—and many of their parents and teachers, who had grown up with the same attitude, showed an obtuse aversion to change. She had seen the damning effects of that combination of factors in the lowered expectations that many of her law students in Fayetteville had held for themselves. They got by, but no better. Hillary knew that if the state's brightest minds were so poisoned, then the state's average and weaker students had to be floundering even more.

"Bringing the idea of education reform to the public was an education process for Arkansas," explains Skip Rutherford, a Little Rock friend and educator who worked with Hillary on the reforms and on the board of Arkansas Children's Hospital. "She helped educate the educators. She said: we can't sit back and let the world go by without us. We're going to have to compete. We must upgrade our educational standards and our educational systems. And it's not going to be done overnight, and change is not easy. But someone's got to take this to the people, to explain why we need this. And she did it. You can't imagine the time and energy it took to go to meeting after meeting, with 'Mrs. Clinton, why do we have to do this?' and 'Why should we do this?' She was very good, very patient. She has a way with people."

"There are advantages to smallness so long as smallness is accompanied by excellence," Hillary told people. And they listened. At a Pulaski County P.T.A. Council Founders Day luncheon, she said, "We expect nothing but the best from our athletes: discipline, teamwork, standards. I wish we could translate the same expectations and standards we have for athletics into the classroom. I wish we could give teachers the same support and praise for teaching children to read and write as we do those who teach them to throw a ball through a hoop."

In a lengthy interview with the *Arkansas Democrat*, she elaborated: "One of the principal problems we face in our state, and apparently in the country, is that we are not expecting enough of ourselves, our schools, or our students. We have an obligation to challenge our students and to set high expectations for them. Rather than setting minimum standards, we should set expectations and urge schools and districts to aim to achieve those expectations and not to be satisfied with meeting some artificial minimum."

Hillary proved once again she knew how to lead. At first she took a backseat in discussions, acting mostly as a moderator and being careful not to dominate the discussion. It took a bit of time for her to master the Arkansas group dynamics. Her old skills as conciliator served her well. As time passed, she became progressively a stronger force, emerging so powerfully after a short time that the panel came informally to be called the "Hillary committee."

A key element in education reform, she believed, was accountability. It would have to work in both directions. Third-, sixth-, and eighth-graders would have to pass minimum-skill competency exams before being promoted. Schools in which more than fifteen percent of students failed exams would have to participate in a state-sponsored improvement program or face the loss of accreditation. Teenagers would have to stay in school until age seventeen. At that time they were able to stop at age sixteen, or after eighth grade.

School time had to be made more valuable if students were to be expected to perform. Hillary was shocked by the paucity of curricular choices available in many of the Arkansas public schools. At her own Maine South High School back home she had been able to choose from a wide range of math and science courses, foreign languages, and advanced-placement classes—programs that aren't offered in many Arkansas schools even today.

"I was exposed to a really broad education," she told the *Arkansas Gazette*, "and it was very difficult for me to understand when I first started working [on educational standards in Arkansas] in 1983 that the vast majority of the students here . . . would never be exposed to what I was exposed to in the fifties and sixties."

The committee's goal was to draft a set of new standards by the 1983–84 school year so that comments could be solicited from the public and written into the final draft. Hillary began to conduct county hearings, traveling from town to town. She went through seventy-five counties—a stellar feat. She stressed that improving education was a consumer issue: parents had the right to demand the best teaching possible for what they were paying with their taxes.

Some of the committee's recommendations, such as a call for smaller classes in kindergarten and elementary schools, were easily accepted. A proposed requirement that high schools offer more courses, including English, math, science, social studies, and fine arts, set well with adult voters if not with teenagers.

Others, like a demand for statewide teacher testing, were less well received. The proposal unleashed a torrent of opposition and the teachers' union geared up for war. One school librarian was quoted as calling Hillary Clinton "lower than a snake's belly." A principal told her he didn't want the children in his district to get an education. The National Education Association fought the test in court but failed.

The governor's legislative package that year included a proposed $180 million tax increase for education. The revenues were to come from a highly controversial sales tax increase. The teachers test, which was popular with parents if not teachers, was a way to make the people of Arkansas feel they were "getting" something—accountability—for their hard-earned tax money. Clinton said he felt "it is a small price to pay for the biggest tax increase in the history of the state and to restore the teaching profession to the position of public esteem that I think it deserves."

The Education Standards Committee officially completed its nearly nine months of work and approved a final version of its proposed new standards for the accreditation of the Arkansas public schools on December 10, 1983. Its report called for a maximum class size of twenty to twenty-five students in most grades, increased curricular requirements, including a half credit in fine arts, lengthening the school year from 175 to 180 days, and the provision of additional student counselors, among other points.

In speeches around the state, and even at a daring venture into a hostile conference of the American Federation of Teachers, Hillary rallied public opinion around the idea of testing teachers to weed out "incompetents." The public perceived that many classroom teachers were incompetent, she argued, "and whether it was fair, whether it was accurate or true, we

were going to have to come to terms with the perceptions that they were," she argued. "The problem and
the perception had to be dealt with together." Hillary
also appreciated the pragmatic need of using the tests
to help voters accept their first sales tax increase in
twenty-six years.

Hillary presented her report on the committee's
findings and recommendations to the Arkansas legislature in a stuffy and crowded committee room on a
hot day in 1983. Opinion on the reforms was, at the
outset, closely divided. Then Hillary made her presentation. A silence fell over the room after she finished.

"I think we've elected the wrong Clinton," state representative Lloyd George of Danville remarked.

"No, the work's too hard," Hillary responded, smiling.

Bill Clinton then sauntered into the meeting. He had
been standing in the state Capitol hallway, peering in
at his wife through the committee room's glass door.
He took a seat next to Democratic state senator Nick
Wilson of Pocahontas. He sat silently, beaming. Hillary
remained in the room to answer questions for over two
hours. She tried to keep it all perfectly official. The advocate in her was again battling with the observer.

The legislators finally pressured her into revealing
some perpetual opinions about education in Arkansas.
Making sure to say she wasn't speaking for the committee, she said she thought that more state money
should be pumped into teacher salary increases. They
kept her there talking until all the issues were talked
through. When it was over, the legislators stood and
applauded.

"They were just melting in her presence, because
she was just so extraordinarily good," Betsey Wright
remembers.

"She carries a lot more weight with some legislators

and a lot of people out there in the state than Bill does, there's no doubt about that," Nick Wilson said. Lloyd George thought a line should be added to "Clinton for Governor" bumper stickers to say, "Hillary, that is."

"You're always getting me in trouble at home," Hillary quipped back.

Eventually she won the public over as well to her proposal to administer standard tests to pupils. Students, she argued, had the right to a good education—and they also had a duty to repay the state for their schooling through good performance. It made for a convincing argument.

The teacher competency tests, however, remained more controversial. The first series was dismissed by critics as laughably easy. They suggested that spending state funds to promote the idea of responsible performance was more important to the committee than actually bringing about change.

With a feeling of having had insult piled onto injury, the Arkansas Education Association attacked the teacher testing law. Association representatives also attacked Bill Clinton, Hillary Clinton, the press, and anyone else who supported the standards. What was to become a protracted feud began. At one hearing, when Dr. Kai Erikson, executive secretary of the AEA, testified, Hillary rolled her eyes, picked up her coat, and left.

Her sarcastic looks and jabs weren't altogether unjustified. There were some ironies in the AEA's attacks. The group was saying that the standards would cost too much and would take away from teachers' salaries. But in 1980 the AEA had proposed a comprehensive Quality Education Act that detractors then had said would be too costly. The group had for years lobbied for the state to make efforts at bettering the schools. Now it was calling for local control. Also, for last few years, the AEA had advocated tax increases for education; after a penny sales tax increase for education, they were saying that the proposed standards were too high, the state was being unrealistic, and was wrongfully trying to do more than it could afford.

On March 23, 1985, Arkansas's more than 25,000 teachers took the competency test. Just the day before, a state court judge had ruled it was not unconstitutional. A threatened teachers' strike did not materialize. But just before the test was to be administered, there were allegations that copies of it had been leaked in advance. The Arkansas Department of Education ended up having to release a statement saying that no compromising practices had taken place.

Ten percent of the state's teachers failed the test. For the most part, they failed the writing portion, which required them to compose two hundred-word essays on various themes, such as a letter to be sent home to a parent or a memo to colleagues that explained a new teaching technique.

Black teachers failed at a much higher rate than whites. Some Arkansas critics charged that the test was blatantly racist—a tool to devalue and oust black teachers or intimidate them into quitting.

"It was a way to appeal to the segregationists by using another symbol for race," a critic says. "When they said they were testing for teacher competency and would get the incompetents out of there, people's heads saw black teachers. And then ten percent of the black teachers were gone after that test, and that test was a joke. It was true that some of them had had difficulty, but mostly it was such a zonker emotionally that they were afraid of it."

The criticism was so forceful that Bill Clinton was moved to make an appearance on the CBS new program *Face the Nation* to say that the test was not discriminatory.

"I don't think he expected it to be," the critic says. "He wasn't thinking about that at all. He was thinking about getting his damn sales tax passed."

Hillary took the ten percent failure rate as a vindication of her committee's efforts. "Nobody should have failed our test," she said to the *Washington Post*. "The fact that ten percent failed is very significant. Those ten percent touch thousands and thousands of children's lives."

Not all educators were won over, however, by her fire and rhetoric. Linda Darling-Hammond, a nationally respected educator, called Arkansas's test "a quick-fix political measure" that was "at worst, counterproductive." As she addressed the American Federation of Teachers, Darling-Hammond, unlike Hillary, was treated to uproarious applause when she made the point that Arkansas ranked fiftieth among the states in education spending, and that the average teacher salary then in some of the state's districts was $12,000.

Despite lingering criticism—and lawsuit threats by the National Education Association—the Arkansas test was followed by similar efforts in Georgia and Texas. In the latter, scores of teachers' union volunteers combed the state tutoring teachers to help them pass. In Arkansas, the state provided opportunities for remedial instruction to the teachers who failed. The tests, it was then argued ultimately, served the purpose of increasing teacher education. Eventually, Hillary's program for "in-service" education of teachers was backed by the teachers' union that had booed her in the first place.

Someone had to eventually criticize Clinton's choice of Hillary. Predictably enough, in the spring of 1984,

Erwin Davis, a Republican gubernatorial hopeful from Fayetteville, accused Bill Clinton of violating state nepotism laws by appointing his wife to head the Education Standards Commission. But the issue did him little good in the election. That year, Hillary Clinton had already received the Arkansas Press Association's first Headliner of the Year award for making good news with her educational reform efforts, among other accolades. It just wasn't an issue that could bring the Governor, or his wife, down.

One major initiative that eventually grew out of Hillary Clinton's work on the standards committee was the establishment in Arkansas of the first Home Instruction Program for Preschool Youngsters program, known as HIPPY. She had learned of the program in 1985 when, while attending a meeting of the Southern Governors' Association in Miami, she had read an article describing it in the *Miami Herald*.

The HIPPY program had been developed in the 1960s at Hebrew University in Jerusalem to help the educationally disadvantaged children of immigrants gain the basic skills they would need to function in mainstream public schools. It differed from programs like Head Start in that it taught mothers to teach their children at home. The idea was to give mothers a sense of responsibility for their children's education, and for teaching other mothers to do the same. The children weren't taught to read and write, but rather to learn the basic concepts necessary to do well in school later. As Hillary explained to Charles Allen: "Half of all learning occurs by the time a person is five. There are instances, each of us knows, where people from very terrible situations rise above them and do well. But those are the exceptions, and most people who have the kind of impoverished, often neglectful backgrounds that we see so often among many of our children today just come into school with so many problems that it's very difficult to deal with. So a good preschool program, whether it's center-based or home-based, is one of the smartest investments. . . . What HIPPY does is to provide a very structured way for mothers to interact with their children. A lot of other programs are well meaning, but they basically put too much responsibility on the mother. If the mother knew what she was supposed to do, she would do it."

By March 1984, Hillary was able to say proudly, "We've turned the corner on attitude."

It was a good year. She and Bill Clinton made the *Esquire* Registry, a list of 272 people the magazine called "the best of the new generation." Also in March, Hillary received the Public Citizen of the Year award from the Arkansas chapter of the National Association of Social Workers. In May she was chosen as Woman of the Year in a poll of *Arkansas Democrat* readers.

"The popularity of that education program during that period of time was unbelievable," the *Arkansas Democrat*'s John Robert Starr remembers. "That was the first time I've ever seen the people of Arkansas asking for a tax increase."

The impact of the education reforms was felt throughout the state for years after Hillary's committee work was done. The HIPPY program grew and expanded, and by 1990 involved two thousand young students. Most important, the state had undergone a real, permanent change in the way it thought about education.

"You can still see the benefits of what she's done because you can go into town after town, county after county, do a survey on what's the number one issue in the area, and it'll be education," Skip Rutherford says. "The single most important thing in my opinion that she did was to make Arkansas believe in themselves, to see that anything is possible, to be proud of their heritage, and to look at it as an asset to have grown up in a small state."

Hillary had achieved what had once seemed impossible: she had found a cause—right in Arkansas—and she had used all her skills and strengths to better people's lives. She had built up the constituency her law school friends had hoped she would find. She'd made a lot of new friends too, great political allies. And now a stream of projects and offers to chair boards and foundations were coming her way. She was hitting her stride. After ten years in Arkansas, she had fully come into her own. Now the state was changing itself for *her*.

Or maybe the two were just growing together. By 1986, Hillary was a pillar of the Little Rock legal establishment, and a fully assimilated member of the city. She had mastered such a southern professional look that in pictures from the period she is almost unrecognizable. Her hair was short and loosely curled, brushed back from her face like a fuller, softer version of Nancy Reagan's. Her legal career had raced along over the years as well. At a firm where two-thirds of the partners had earned their law degrees at the University of Arkansas, Hillary easily stood out. She developed Rose's intellectual-property and patent-infringement practice. She gained renown for being the first trial lawyer in the state to conduct an examination by satellite of a witness who was unable to travel to the trial. In 1989, a survey of Arkansas's top lawyers named her one of the best business-litigation attorneys in the state.

Thomas Mars, a partner at Stanley, Harrington and Mars in Springdale, Arkansas, who worked for Hillary as an associate during his first year out of law school, remembers her as a skillful litigator who worked past midnight on occasion, taking depositions and polishing written reports. She was a perfectionist, he says, as well as a hard-driving employer, but she also had a skill in the courtroom that was edifying to behold. One oral argument in particular stands out in his mind. Hillary was pleading the case of a father who wanted to wrest custody of his child away from his wife, a difficult case in any state and particularly tough to argue then in Arkansas.

"I can still picture her standing there with her palms down on the table, getting ready to deliver her closing argument," Mars says. "It had just gotten dark outside, there were more spectators than usual in the courtroom, and you could've heard a pin drop. She delivered a closing argument that lasted fifteen or twenty minutes that was really emotional and extremely articulate. She didn't have notes, as usual for Hillary, and she never missed a beat. The judge ruled from the bench and granted a change of custody."

"She always argues from the heart," her friend Nancy Snyderman says.

There were always, especially during an election year, periodic claims that Hillary Clinton's name helped the Rose Law Firm gain state business, but there has never been any real proof of this. Rose, Arkansas's second largest law firm, representing the major financial powers of the state, ranked fifth on the list of firms receiving state contracts a few years ago. Under the terms of her partnership, Hillary shared none of the money the firm earned from state contracts and received no fees from representing bond underwriters. The proximity of business and government was so common in Arkansas anyway that her work raised few eyebrows before the partisan boxing of the presidential campaign began. Her partner, Webb Hubbell, had actually served as mayor of Little Rock from 1979 to 1981. Arkansas had its own rules, and anybody who played by them was usually safe from censure.

The first half of the decade wasn't all triumph, however. In 1984, during Bill Clinton's second term as governor, a colonel of the state police called his office to say that Roger Clinton, the Governor's twenty-seven-year-old stepbrother, had been seen selling cocaine and was now under surveillance. They were planning to arrest him, but wanted the Governor's approval. Bill approved, in perhaps the most painful decision of his life.

Roger Clinton served more than a year in prison. After he stopped using cocaine, he discovered that his real problem was alcoholism, like his father. Bill, Roger, their mother, and occasionally Hillary were called in for intensive family therapy. They discussed co-dependency. Hillary took a leading role in the discussions, and was quite astute at pointing out patterns and weaknesses to the assembled family.

"That was incredibly cathartic for them. Hillary was really one of the first to open up and talk about what she saw as some of the vulnerabilities of that family," Kris Rogers says. "She's very good at capturing what's going on in people's hearts and minds, sometimes saying it for them better than they can themselves. I think she does that for Bill a lot."

Both Bill and Roger Clinton, looking back on that time years later, saw it as a period of great leaps in self-knowledge and growth. But it was painful at the time, and often unpleasant. It was hard for Hillary too. She had to walk a fine line between telling the family things they didn't want to hear and stepping on too many toes. Though he was grateful afterward, her participation didn't always endear her at the time to her husband.

A first encounter with psychotherapy, and the ghosts of the past, can be extremely destabilizing. Therapy forced Bill to look inside himself, at the darkness that so often threatened to trip him up. Like many extremely friendly, outgoing people, he was unused to that kind of introspection. Friends of the Clintons have said they believed that the period of soul-searching shook him up quite a bit. Published reports have suggested that it affected his marriage, for a short while. Turning forty was also rough territory, as it is for many men.

"I was forty when I was sixteen" is a statement he has made many times to explain his eruption of adolescent behavior at the later date. Perhaps it was that the arrest of his half brother, making public the trouble in his family, opened old wounds. Perhaps facing up to the troubles in his life made him cede to them. Friends have said that Bill began to see himself as a failure around this time, that his mood fell and he became self-destructive. Once again the rumor mill started up with stories of adulterous affairs.

Reporters zoomed in on Clinton's outside activities and found nothing credible. And, it is said, his family and close friends did their best to close in around him, shielding him from the public eye, and from the gaze of those who would have been quick to exploit his weakness. In the wake of the media scandal-mongering of 1992, that close circle still stands tight, lips shut.

Kris Rogers, however, retains the impression that therapy actually pulled Bill and Hillary Clinton more solidly together. "That was one of the real watersheds for them," she says. "I think it made her feel closer to Bill."

To this day he still reads books and medical studies

on children of alcoholics, perhaps searching for something that will shed light on the obscure pain within him. Roger Clinton, fully rehabilitated, became a production assistant in Burbank for Harry Thomason and Linda Bloodworth-Thomason, creators and producers of *Designing Women, Evening Shade,* and *Hearts Afire.* He also plays in a rhythm and blues band, Politics, and sometimes performs around town.

In 1986, Hillary received a grant from the Winthrop Rockefeller Foundation to develop a program that would help "at-risk" children with social, psychological, or economic problems improve their chances in school. In November of that year, she was named to the William T. Grant Foundation Commission on Work, Family and Citizenship to compile a study on "Youth and America's Future." She was also that month appointed to the board of directors of Wal-Mart, Inc., of Bentonville. Meanwhile, Bill Clinton was running yet again for governor. There had been a contested primary, against Orval Faubus, among other opponents. Frank White, who had won his last race through personal attacks on the Clintons, was running on the Republican ticket, and the 1986 race promised to be ugly as well.

Chelsea was too big now not to understand campaign slurs on TV, too little to realize they weren't necessarily true, but old enough to know that rock-slinging hurt. Hillary and Bill decided they had to begin to educate her in the seamier side of political life.

"When I saw we were going to have a primary campaign in 1986, Bill and I talked to her at dinner, telling her that sometimes in political campaigns, people say mean and untrue things about other people. And her eyes got real big, and she said, 'Like what?' And I said, 'Why don't you pretend to be your daddy?' She was six years old. 'Why should you be governor?' And she said, 'I should be governor because I've done a good job.' And I said, 'Okay, but somebody running against your daddy will stand up and say, 'Bill Clinton has done a terrible job, he doesn't care about anybody, he's a bad person.' Her eyes just got huge. And she said, 'Why would they say that?' And I said, 'Because they want people to vote for them," Hillary told the *Washington Post*.

Gay White and Hillary Clinton were also pitted against each other. In the local press, Mrs. White accused Hillary of being a first lady who "shamelessly uses" her "vicarious role." Frank White accused her of conflict of interest because she benefited financially from bond business done with the state by the Rose Law Firm. On a morning talk radio show, he claimed she had made $500,000. The Rose Law Firm had served as either bond counsel or underwriter's counsel on every bond issue by the Arkansas Development Finance Authority, an agency that had played a key role in the governor's economic-development program since 1983. Clinton acknowledged his wife had benefited financially, but denied a conflict-of-interest problem. According to the *Arkansas Democrat*, calculations based on figures provided by the ADFA showed that the entire Rose firm had received only $159,000 for serving as bond counsel on six of twenty bond issues for the three years proceeding.

Finally, Hillary challenged White to reveal his own earnings from state-related business while employed at Stephens, Inc., the major investment-banking firm located in Little Rock, and said that she would release her own earnings from bond business. She and Governor Clinton offered to disclose their tax returns, but Frank and Gay White refused.

To counter the Whites' negative attacks, Clinton

based much of his campaign on extolling the work that Hillary had done in education since 1983. The phrase *two for one* was first used in reference to Bill and Hillary just after the 1986 election, for many voters told reporters they had voted for the Governor because it would mean electing his wife too. In his victory speech, Bill thanked her for standing by him so staunchly. "I'm proud that she made this walk with me tonight," he said to applause that seemed to surpass his own reception. "I think when the history of our state is written . . . no one will prove to have done more to advance the cause of our children and the future of this state than she has."

This was the golden age of Bill and Hillary Clinton's reign over the state of Arkansas. They were frantically busy. Hillary's typical day, after work at the law firm, might include a conference, a cocktail reception at the governor's mansion, a museum-exhibition opening, and a dinner party, with her first meal after a vending-machine lunch eaten at nearly ten o'clock at night. Often for dinner she merely sneaked hors-d'oeuvres in the kitchen during an official reception. Time with Bill was hard to catch. Hillary might wait up late at night for him, if she could. Otherwise they saw each other while riding together in the limousine between events.

They made every effort they could to find time together to relax and reconnect. Making personal time was essential to Hillary. It was so easy to be devoured by the governorship, to have no time left for a married life, a personal life, a social life.

"Our social life is almost nonexistent," she told the *Arkansas Gazette* in 1986, "We love going to friends for a visit, but we seldom do it. Maybe once a month, if that often."

She always, however, made time for Chelsea. Her daughter was a pleasure. When she began school, Hillary drove her in the mornings, savoring that time spent together. She kept mementos and little presents that Chelsea made her—like a plastic bead necklace of beautiful "jewels" she fashioned once in Washington after seeing the jewelry many of the other wives wore. Hillary wore the necklace to a formal lunch the next day. If the limousine driver thought anything odd of it, he didn't say. Chelsea was very proud.

Hillary Clinton was asked in 1986 if she had any plans of her own for political races any time in the future. She said that she had no personal political ambitions. "I'll let Bill do that. I value being a private person too much," she told the *Gazette*. What she didn't say was that Bill Clinton was considering running for president. It was the dream of his lifetime.

The preliminary campaign machinery was set in place. Phone calls were made, advisers considered. Hillary braced herself for what she knew would be a messy race. She braced Chelsea. She was excited, though. She was going to have a shot at being first lady of the nation.

A press conference was called in Little Rock for July 15, 1987. All indications were that Bill Clinton was about to announce his candidacy for the presidency. There were subtle and not-so-subtle clues. The Clintons had just recently bought a condo for Hillary's parents in the Cantrell Road area of Little Rock, presumably so that they could keep a close eye on Chelsea while the Clintons were out on the road.

Dozens of reporters and guests of the Governor's flew into Little Rock. Some had come for his scheduled announcement luncheon at the mansion. Others brought their gear to cover the press conference. Everyone was ready to go. The news conference had been scheduled eight days earlier, and the general belief was that Clinton would use it to announce his formation of an exploratory committee for the election. The grand ballroom of the Excelsior Hotel was filled to capacity, jammed with network TV crews and people from all over the country. But then something went wrong. The Governor and those close to him, the honored guests from the luncheon, looked as though they were in the grips of a powerful emotion—a bad one. It turned out that over chicken salad in the mansion dining room, he had made the announcement that he wouldn't be running. He and Hillary had discussed the fact that they knew the campaign would bury them in rumors of his infidelity, he said, and they had decided it wasn't worth it, not then. Chelsea was only seven.

Tears rising in his eyes, Bill Clinton officially announced he would not seek the nomination. "My heart says no," he said at an hour-long news conference. "Our daughter is seven. She is the most important person in the world to us and our most important responsibility. In order to wage a winning campaign, both Hillary and I would have to leave her for long periods of time. That would not be good for her or for us."

As he spoke of his promise to himself, "a long, long time ago . . . if I was ever lucky enough to have a kid, my child would never grow up wondering who her father was," Hillary brushed a tear from her face.

He had changed his mind, he said, a good seven days earlier, but had delayed the announcement until the Tuesday news conference because it would "give me enough time to change my mind, if I could change it."

"It was shocking and it was very moving," says Max Brantley, editor of the *Arkansas Times*. "The room was jammed with network TV crews and people from all over the country. And most of the people and friends of Bill's and political associates in the room fully expected him to announce that he was running for president. It was one of the most moving talks he had ever given. He didn't speak from notes, he spoke from his heart. It seemed a really genuine performance. It seemed regretful on his part and deeply felt, and it seemed that he had a high purpose. I guess it was the picture of a politician forgoing a chance to do something that clearly, from the day I met him, I knew he was destined to do. It seemed a selfless kind of decision."

That night, a group of Bill and Hillary's friends threw a party. Carolyn Staley made a banner reading "WELCOME HOME, BILL" and had a professional sign maker color it red, white, and blue. She hung it on the front of her house to welcome the Clintons back home.

Both Bill and Hillary delivered measured, intellectualized statements afterward about not running. Hillary made the most of a bad situation by calling the media coverage of Gary Hart and other politicians' private lives a "return to an assessment of values." Expanding on one of her favorite themes, she called the issue a "symptom, an indicator of a large question," involving people "casting about, looking for models and examples. We've really lost our way," she told the *Arkansas Democrat.* "It's very tough to lead a satisfying life these days. . . . And so I see all these stories or allegations, or whatever they are, as desperate attempts on the part of the press, frankly, to really figure out what's going on underneath. . . . What's really going on is . . . people deciding to spend more time with their children . . . to gain some balance. . . . What's going on is real interesting, but no one is writing about it. Nobody understands it yet."

The rambling explanation did little more to hide her

pain than Bill Clinton's blunt admission to the *New York Times*: "It hurt so bad to walk away from it."

Bill had spoken to Gary Hart on the phone that summer. The depth of attention the candidate from Colorado had received, and the extent of the probe into his personal life, had deeply shaken Clinton. Afterward, sitting and watching one of Chelsea's softball games with Max Brantley, he sadly shook his head.

"You know," he said reflectively, speaking almost to an invisible audience somewhere out in the ball field before him, "is there a point ever in a person's life, a political person's life, when the things you've done in the past are forgotten? There's nobody in the world who hasn't done things they weren't embarrassed about. Aren't you ever forgiven? Aren't they ever allowed to be in the past?"

In the context of a conversation about Gary Hart, it seems fair to assume that Bill Clinton was talking about absolution by the public, by the country. But with hindsight one can't help but wonder whether he was speaking just as much about Hillary.

That the Clintons had fairly severe marital difficulties at that time appears to be confirmed by his statement to Steve Kroft: "If we had given up on our marriage . . . three years ago, four years ago, you know . . . if we were divorced, I wouldn't be half the man I am today, without her and Chelsea." What really happened in private, in discussions between Bill and Hillary at that time, as in 1984 and 1980 and whenever else they may, like all married couples, have had difficulties, will never be known. Hillary's commitment to preserving a "zone of privacy" in their lives is unswerving, and the few friends with whom she has discussed the difficulties will never betray that trust. She is, furthermore, extremely circumspect, and has confided fully in few of her friends. As she told *Newsweek*:

"What is important to us is that we have always dealt with each other. We haven't run away or walked away. We've been willing to work through all kinds of problems. You have hard times because people overwork and they get short-tempered. Marriages go through rough times because you have problems with family members like we've had. It's very stressful. There are all kinds of things that happen. And I think it is inappropriate to talk about that. I don't believe in all of that confessional stuff, because from my perspective you begin to undermine the relationship when you open it up to strangers. We don't talk about this kind of stuff in our marriage with family and friends. It's the way we are and how we live. And I think it's the way most people live."

Even if Hillary Clinton had spoken to friends, it is unlikely that her confidences would have been detailed, personally involved anecdotes full of emotional outpourings of grief. That's just not what she's like as a friend.

"She's always more interested in helping you than she is in asking for help," Nancy Snyderman says. "Even at times I think might have been rocky in her life, she does not say, 'Help me fix my life.' She doesn't put her life out there for everyone to sample." Such admissions would also not be typical of the way she handles emotion in her life.

"Hillary has a great ability to take her personal feelings and put them in a soft cushion and set them back in the back of her head while she goes on and not let them interfere," Betsy Wright says.

That's a somewhat suspect quality, if an admirable one, as back-burner feelings usually burst into flame at some point. One would think that Hillary Clinton could not, despite her work, despite her family, despite her church, have avoided experiencing altogether the pain that Bill said he caused in the marriage. But that is conjecture. Similarly, most of the stories of what passed between them that have been reported or discussed so far are, for the most part, conjecture. Discussions of their marriage have become something of a cottage industry, just like story-selling was for Gennifer Flowers. The theories range from the rather mundane to the highly creative. They include the belief that the Clintons once had an "open marriage," where both were free to pursue affairs. These fictions, stated as fact, make up the bulk of a growing body of Clinton lore, and stem from sources as wide-ranging as John Robert Starr to *Vanity Fair* to the *National Enquirer*, not to mention countless gossips too numerous to mention.

Starr's story is quite elaborate:

"My theory on Bill Clinton's love affair," he says, "is that in the term when he was out of office, or certainly when he was defeated, he thought he had fallen in love. Not with Gennifer Flowers. And I don't think it was a casual fling, a one-night deal. I don't think it lasted very long, though. I think that in 1987, when Bill was thinking about the presidency and the Gary Hart thing came up, he realized that he was going to be asked the same questions and he bowed out, not because Chelsea was seven years old—going to the White House will damage a seven-year-old child a hell of a lot less than it will damage an eleven-year-old child—he dropped out because he hadn't told Hillary. And he realized that if this came out during the campaign, and if Hillary left him, he would be dead meat, just like he would have been dead meat this year if Hillary hadn't stood by him. I think he then told her the whole truth. It would have been stupid not to. By then it was all over. I think he told her the truth, and I don't think she would have stuck by him if there had been a whole bunch of women.

"Reports are that this was a very stormy time. That her feelings were deeply hurt, as any woman's would be. Because she's not the cold, completely calculating total political machine that they've tried to make her out to be."

Starr's theory has provoked cackles of laughter from Hillary's friends and angry denunciations too.

"Sounds like Bob Starr got taken off his leash one day—he had rabies—and he's still out there; he didn't die, he's just mean," Connie Fails says.

Other friends dispute the idea that the Clintons ever had anything approaching an open marriage. They never were separated, they note, and certainly never had the privacy—in Little Rock, of all places—to live out an alternative form of marriage that many of Clinton's constituents would have found inappropriate. "They've not been people who lived two separate lives at any time or appeared to me to be sticking together solely for public purposes," Ellen Brantley says.

Through all the troubled points in their marriage, the Clintons have said repeatedly, the couple did not consider divorce. Hillary stumbled a bit in saying so when talking to David Frost.

"Not seriously," she said when Frost asked if they'd ever mentioned the word *divorce*.

"No, no," she said, "I mean—I never doubted and I know he never did either, that not only do we love each other, but that we were committed to each other. That that love was something so much a part of us that it was impossible to think of ending it or cutting it off or moving beyond it."

By the time she talked to *Glamour* in the late summer, she was more definitive: "Bill and I have always loved each other," she said. "No marriage is perfect, but just because it isn't perfect doesn't mean the only solution is to walk off and leave it. A marriage is always growing and changing. We couldn't say, 'Well, this isn't ideal' and get a divorce. I'm proud of my marriage. I have women friends who chose not to marry, or who married and chose not to have children, or who married and then divorced, or who had children on their own. That's okay, that's their choice. This is my choice. This is how I define my personhood—Bill and Chelsea."

"They both wanted their marriage. They went through the hard work it takes to get beyond that," Betsey Wright says. "It was not an open marriage. It's not that they sit around and tolerate each other running around. It takes really hard work to heal the wounds in a relationship following infidelity. It's like medicine, and it's like therapy, physical therapy and mental therapy, and they went through that, and it was worth it. And I think their marriage is stronger for it. I think that they, in the process, were able to articulate what was valuable about each other, and you know, I have a lot of friends whose marriages are solid, but it's routine. And it's not routine to Bill and Hillary. With them, it's almost a fresh new commitment."

It does seem, from all accounts, that the Clinton marriage emerged happier and healthier after the infidelity issues had been worked through than possibly it had ever been before. "We just had to deal with the issues in our marriage and work them out," Hillary told *People*.

The image of those two passionate people hashing out these issues is a poignant one. The question of what Chelsea must have seen or heard is a painful one too. A rather amusing answer was provided, however, by the *National Enquirer* in December. In an issue that also featured an article headlined, "NEW WHITE HOUSE CAT FACES NERVOUS BREAKDOWN—THE UNTOLD STORY," and featured pictures of a rather alarmed-looking

Socks, wearing leash, collar, and bells, the *Enquirer* revealed "NEW FIRST LADY'S INTIMATE SECRETS" like that a nine-year-old Chelsea had sobbed, "Mommy, why doesn't Daddy love you anymore?" just days after Christmas in 1989, and had moved Hillary to do something about her marriage. The article revealed, through an unnamed "friend," that Hillary, having ignored repeated rumors of Bill's affairs and having "grown so far apart that I didn't think the marriage would survive," took "desperate" steps that year, including seeing a marriage counselor, consulting with her minister (where both cried)—and buying sexy lingerie. The story's best point came when an unnamed "source at the governor's mansion" related, "Their rows used to get pretty loud. On one occasion Hillary and Bill got into a fight at his office—and when she came storming out, he stood at the top of the stairs yelling: 'I'm still the governor here, bitch, and don't you forget it!' " Rumors that Socks sold that story to the *Enquirer* have yet to be confirmed.

After the painful summer of 1987, life went on for the Clintons much as before. In the fall Hillary was active in working as a member of a special committee appointed by U.S. District Judge Henry Woods to find a way to eliminate racially identifiable schools— schools with enrollments of seventy-five percent black or greater. Also that year, Robert MacCrate, a retired partner with Sullivan and Cromwell in New York and then president of the American Bar Association, appointed Hillary Clinton as the first chairperson of the newly created twelve-member ABA Commission on Women and the Profession. Up until that time, the participation of women in the ABA had been very limited. This was a chance to place women's issues into the mainstream of ABA activity, and bring women more fully into the group's activities. Hillary had the idea of inventorying each section of the ABA to see how many women were participating in them and at what level. She conducted hearings to listen to the problems that women had encountered in law firms, in the courts, in legal education. From these hearings reports were prepared. "Hillary was able to stimulate all sorts of constructive developments within the association that have significantly changed the course of the constituency of the association." The ABA, said MacRate, "used to be a very male-dominated old boys' club." As a result of her work, MacRate thinks the participation of women in the ABA has greatly increased.

"People have told me that the best appointment I ever made was Hillary as chairman of that commission," he says.

In 1988, the Clintons jointly received the National Humanitarian Award from the National Conference of Christians and Jews. Mayor Andrew Young of Atlanta spoke in praise of them at the Little Rock meeting and said that their partnership, based upon a commitment to public service and to each other, was a model other couples would have to emulate if marriage was to survive in the future.

In 1989, Hillary Clinton accompanied her husband to the presidential education summit at the University of Virginia. She attended the meetings but, as a spouse, was not allowed to participate. She did, however, have a word or two to say to her table neighbor, George Bush, at a luncheon one day.

"You know, Mr. President," she said, "depending upon what statistic you look at, we're at seventeenth or eighteenth in the whole world in infant mortality."

"Hillary, whatever are you talking about?" he responded, according to her account to Sam Donaldson last year. "Our health-care system is the envy of the world."

"Not if you want to keep your child alive to the year of his first birthday," she answered. She told Bush she would go back to her hotel room that night and get the statistics and have Bill Clinton give them to him the next day.

"I'll get my own statistics," he said.

The next day Bush handed Bill Clinton a note. It read: "Tell Hillary she was right."

Betsey Wright resigned that year. She said it was due to exhaustion, but staffers close to her whispered there had been a falling out between her and the Governor—something having to do with the abrupt way she dealt with many state legislators. Other rumors held that the fight had been between Wright and Hillary.

Jerry Russell, a political consultant in Little Rock, said he had been told by a lobbyist—unnamed—that Wright had had a "serious difference of opinion" with Hillary over whether Clinton should seek reelection. "Hillary thinks Bill ought to run for reelection and Betsey doesn't," Russell told a group of business, industrial, and government leaders from all across the state. Although in a recent interview he called his assertion "an opinion rather than a statement of fact," his words did contribute to creating an atmosphere of tension in the Clinton camp at that time, and reinforced certain local suspicions about the power-brokering and infighting behind the throne in the Clinton administration.

The issue was whether or not Bill Clinton would run for office again. Voters were bound to suspect that he'd want to run for president in 1992. That would mean he'd desert them in the middle of his first four-year term (the Arkansas legislature had extended the term for its governor from two to four years). Clinton was evasive in answering questions about whether he was running again. He said at an awards luncheon that he was planning to and then called it a "slip of the tongue."

As the 1990 campaign year began, Hillary Clinton was mentioned as a candidate for Second District representative for Congress. She was supported by Jim Guy Tucker, the former Democratic representative from the district. "It could be very helpful to Bill's eventual ambitions," he said. He added, however, that he had heard no discussion of the issue by Hillary.

At the apex of her popularity, in 1989, there were serious rumors that Hillary herself might run for governor instead of her husband the next year. The Clintons, who have since strongly denied such stories, did little at the time to make them die. In August, Bill told local newspapers that his wife would be "wonderful," "unbelievably good," and "terrific" as governor. But he wouldn't say if she was willing to run if he decided not to run for reelection. "I'm not going to speak for her," he told reporters. "That's not my business." He said that if Hillary was willing to run, "that would have a big impact on my own decision" about whether to seek the governorship again.

The *Arkansas Democrat*'s Meredith Oakley gave her rather acerbic support to the idea of a Hillary Clinton candidacy. Reaffirming the rumors as fact, she wrote, "She wouldn't be the first strong, capable, brilliant woman to stand aside for a weaker, less capable, less brilliant husband."

The idea of running Hillary for governor was taken very seriously indeed. Whit Stephens, the legendary financier, let it ring through the halls at Stephens Inc., his investment bank. He liked it. Finally, the idea started to appeal to Hillary.

"Very briefly, Hillary entertained the idea of running," Max Brantley says. "It's certainly true that some people floated the notion. I think it intrigued her briefly. There was too much said about it to think that it wasn't at least momentarily considered with some degree of seriousness."

Hillary Clinton has assiduously and pointedly denied all the rumors.

"Since I was in eighth grade, people have been urging me to run for public office," she told *Glamour*. People think that because I care so much about public issues, I should run for office myself. I don't want to run for office. In 1990, when it looked as though Bill might not run for governor, I had dozens of people call me and tell me to run. But it just wasn't anything I was interested in. An elected official has to deal with many things—I see the way Bill does it. Seven or eight different things in one day. And he's good at that. What I see for myself is a role as an advocate."

But Brantley sticks by the rumors. "The device in Arkansas is for the politician to say, 'My friends have encouraged me to do this or friends are asking me to do that,' but it's always been my experience that friends never encourage unless you send some signal that you wanted to be encouraged in the first place. That gave you cover to explore the possibilities. I don't think this thing lasted very long, I think it was a real short trial balloon, but there's no question that it got floated."

"We've all encouraged her to run for office," says Ann Henry, the Clintons' Fayetteville friend. "I do think that she once had the opportunity to make a name for herself and run on her own. But once she came to Arkansas, to Bill Clinton's terrain, she had to give up running herself. If Bill had at any point thought of not doing it, though, I know that people would have gone to Hillary."

Whether or not Hillary Clinton could ever have won

an election in Arkansas is rather doubtful. Although her work on educational reform and health care was extremely popular in the state, there was always a certain degree of resistance to her, and some hard core opposition as well. Bill Clinton's natural detractors—Republicans—repudiated her, if politely, and the state's rather powerful religious right viewed her marital role as flying in the face of Scripture. "A rare, small and nutty number" made it their personal campaign to take her on one, Max Brantley says. Other opposition was more mundane, but more widespread as well. "Outspoken, aggressive women who can stand up on their own two feet and get along in the world just leave some people cold," says Brantley. "She's friendly, she's accessible, but she doesn't project the same puppy dog warmth that Bill does. She's threatening to a lot of people in Arkansas."

It was certainly true that in the course of her varying campaigns, Hillary Clinton acquired a reputation with some people for being pushy, arrogant, and domineering. This criticism flared in 1990, when she crashed a press conference being given by an erstwhile friend and political opponent, Tom McRae.

While Bill Clinton was in Washington, McRae, a top challenger in the Democratic primary, called a news conference to criticize him on some points that he said Clinton hadn't adequately answered: teacher salaries, the Vertac dioxin contamination in Jacksonville, clear-cutting, and whether he planned to seek higher office during his next term if reelected. Arkansas, he reminded the crowd, ranked fiftieth among states in teacher pay seven years after the Clintons pushed through the school standards and an accompanying one-cent sales tax increase to pay for them.

"Those are the four issues that I would raise, but since the Governor is not here, I would give him at least an opportunity to respond," McRae said, pointing to a cartoon of Clinton, clothes scattered at his feet, with the caption: "THE EMPEROR HAS NO CLOTHES." Since the Governor will not debate me, we are giving our own answers," he said.

Hillary Clinton, who claimed she just happened to have been at the Capitol "to pick some things up," shot out from the background. She was looking very telegenic, in a houndstooth tweed blazer and turtleneck, with pearl earrings and a big Clinton button on her lapel.

"Do you really want an answer, Tom? Do you really want a response from Bill when you know he's in Washington doing work for the state? That sounds a bit like a stunt to me."

McRae claimed that Clinton had refused to debate him one-on-one.

"Tom, who's the one who didn't show up at the debate in Springdale? Give me a break," Hillary countered.

McRae claimed a scheduling mixup had made him the only Democratic candidate out of five to miss a debate two weeks earlier.

Cameras swinging from McRae to her, she pulled out and began quoting from a four-page prepared statement listing excerpts from reports from the Winthrop Rockefeller Foundation, a public policy institute, that had been issued during the fourteen years McRae had presided over it. Many of the excerpts praised Clinton on the same issues McRae had been lately critical of him, including the environment, economic development, and educational reform. Hillary Clinton had served with McRae on the foundation's board.

"I went through all your reports because I've really been disappointed in you as a candidate, and I've really been disappointed in you as a person, Tom," she said.

McRae acknowledged he had approved or written the reports. He said Clinton's record was in fact good in many areas.

"The issue is not whether he's done good things," McRae finally said. "The final issue is, shouldn't somebody else be given a chance to try? If the best he can do is last, then it's time for someone else to give it a try."

Hillary ticked off Clinton's record of progress. She admitted that problems remained still, but added, "For goodness sakes, let Arkansas stand up and be proud."

McRae remained at the podium, but he was flustered. Clearly the news conference had gotten out of hand. He mentioned a national report from earlier that month that said state education efforts had stagnated.

"It's not that we're not making progress," he said. "It's that we're staying the same."

The cameras kept swinging back and forth. McRae kept smiling. Hillary Clinton did not. She was furious, she said later, about the fact that McRae had displayed a caricature drawing of her husband, nude, with his hands positioned over his crotch.

McRae then said Clinton had reneged on a 1986 campaign pledge to clean up the dioxin spill at Vertac in Jacksonville, which the federal Environmental Protection Agency had listed as one of the worst cases of contamination in the country. He also challenged Clinton's record on trying to put a stop to the incineration of toxic wastes.

"Bill Clinton has never been accused of not being cautious where issues affecting people's health and the environment are concerned," Hillary responded.

Hillary later admitted that she might have heard about McRae's planned news conference when she had spoken at a lunchtime civic club with two other Democratic gubernatorial hopefuls. She claimed, however, to have forgotten about it until she showed up at one-thirty at the Capitol—coincidentally—and a reporter brought it to her attention. She said the notes she had with her were background information she had brought with her to an appearance before the North Little Rock Sertoma Club.

After the McRae-Clinton confrontation, U.S. Representative Tommy Robinson, who had unsuccessfully sought the Republican nomination, said that Hillary had been the real governor of Arkansas for ten years. As former director of public safety during the governor's first term, he told the *Arkansas Gazette*, he had "had to put up with her tirades before." In later interviews with the *Gazette*, he tempered his words, though only obliquely. "As someone who worked in the governor's first administration, I know of times when Mrs. Clinton made the tough decisions that others did not have the courage to make."

"She had no right interrupting his press conference," he told the *Arkansas Democrat*. "It would be just like my wife going to Sheffield Nelson's press conference and lecturing him. . . . If my wife did what Hillary Clinton did," he said, "she and I would have a private discussion."

Robinson had little to fear on that score, however. His wife did not mince words in her opinion of Hillary Clinton's actions. "I hope that I would not do that," she told the *Arkansas Gazette*. "I would hope that I would be able to contain my feelings. I think it's more tasteful to do that. I have to admit, there have been times I'd like to stomp my feet and scream when Tommy has been attacked by some of his opponents and critics, but that's just not my nature."

Meredith Oakley suggested that Bill Clinton lacked

"not only . . . fire in the belly but steel in the spine," and accused him of sending his wife "to do his dirty work." Two days later, however, Oakley, reputedly a feminist, expressed a grudging admiration for the way Hillary Clinton "set out to eat McRae's lunch and didn't stop until she'd finished off his dessert."

"If it were a man," Hillary told the *Gazette*, "they would probably say what a great, strong person this fellow is, how commanding he is and all the rest. . . . I'm not reluctant to say what's on my mind, and if some people interpret that one way instead of another, I can't help that."

The incident seemed to spawn a much more angry reaction in the press than Hillary ever received from Tom McRae himself.

"She was aggressive, but she wasn't obnoxious," McRae says. "My name recognition more than doubled in the next three days. I mean, I was having trouble getting the front page of the Arkansas section of the papers, much less coverage on television, and when the Governor's wife invades a news conference, it sure as hell made me front-page news. After that, the press took my candidacy a lot more seriously. My name recognition went from somewhere in the mid-twenties or so to right at fifty percent. And, in point of fact, I ended up with forty percent of the vote in a six-person race. And I would say that that event was the single biggest publicity shot that I got in the whole campaign."

He now describes Hillary as "friends." "We go back a long way," he says.

During the 1990 campaign for governor, rumors about Clinton's marital infidelities were once again on the rise. The Gary Hart fiasco had left the media hungry for stories about the sexual lives of politicians. Larry Nichols, a former state employee who had been fired two years before for having made fund-raising calls for the contras from his office, filed suit against Clinton, supposedly to get his job back. The lawsuit, however, accused Clinton of having had affairs with five women. Gennifer Flowers was one of them.

The local media had reported the lawsuit, but with little fanfare. Neither the women nor the exact charges had been made explicit. Nelson wasn't considered a reliable source. Both the *Arkansas Democrat* and the *Gazette* did put teams of reporters on the story, but none turned up anything substantial. All five women denied having had affairs with Clinton. Gennifer Flowers even threatened to sue a radio station that had used her name in connection with the lawsuit.

As always, Hillary had to run against the wife of the Republican gubernatorial challenger, Sheffield Nelson. When asked whether his wife, Mary Lynn, would be allowed to "run the state like Hillary," Nelson answered proudly to the contrary. His wife, he said, would be "at the house."

All this had little impact on the campaign. Bill Clinton had his ups and downs. But Hillary as first lady of Arkansas was a sure win.

In honor of the Gulf War, she wore an old dress to the 1991 inaugural ball. It seemed an unauspicious start for the year. But by summer things had perked up. Hillary was involved in a major trial, and Bill was just about deciding to run for president.

Max Brantley recalls a conversation he had with Bill in the early summer of 1991, when both men were at the airport, seeing their children off to summer camp. Clinton, he said, was on the verge of a decision about whether or not to run for president in 1992. Hillary, Brantley says, was strongly pushing him to run. "I don't think they were thinking so much of actually winning in '92 but of using the election for the future, for building up recognition," he says.

It was a tense time, though Hillary's friends would never have known it. Connie Fails, who had one adopted daughter and had fallen in love with a baby girl in Thailand she wanted to bring to Arkansas too, tells the story of how, when it looked as though her adoption was going to fall through, she called Hillary with an urgent request for a letter of recommendation to the agency. She was told that Hillary was out of town. She left a message saying it was urgent. She had thirty-six hours before the child was going to fall out of her hands forever.

Hillary called back as soon as she got the message.

"I have to get the best and biggest letters I can, recommending us as parents," Connie said. "There's another family that wants the child."

Tell me about the child, Hillary said.

She's four years old, Connie Fails said. She's in an orphanage in Thailand.

And, she said, she doesn't have any arms.

There was no response for a moment from the other end of the line.

Where are you? Connie said.

"I'm at a pay phone in the Kansas City Airport, crying," Hillary responded.

"Don't cry for this kid, she's really tough," said Connie.

"I just love you so much," Hillary said.

The letter was ready and waiting at the governor's mansion the next morning.

"I later found out," Fails says, "she was in the middle of the biggest trial of her entire career. It was ten days before Bill announced his candidacy. And she never said anything."

Later that summer, Hillary wrote a letter to her old Wellesley mentor, Alan Schechter. "We are about to start a great adventure," it said.

The word would prove inadequate in the extreme.

6

The 1992 Campaign

January 1992 was by all accounts the best and the worst of times for Hillary Rodham Clinton. For her husband's presidential campaign, the campaign she had poured herself into, body and soul, matters could not have been worse. Bill Clinton was under constant assault, his integrity and southern style assailed, both by Jerry Brown and his youthful followers and by Paul Tsongas, the principled New Englander whose stoic appearance could have made anyone with some style slick by comparison.

Clinton, whose status as a front runner was then held by only shaky and uneven leads in the polls, had for a long time known that his campaign was built over quicksand. The rumors that had dogged him throughout the 1980s, and surfaced with such particular nastiness in the 1990 campaign, were not likely to die. The state of Arkansas itself was a political liability when its vital statistics were turned against him by his Democratic primary opponents. The state he loved was gaining renewed renown as the poorest and, allegedly, most corrupt state in the union, with a highly conservative, back-room-operating legislature, and a poorly educated, mostly rural, politically unsophisticated voting body. Everyone knew that the governor and state legislators of Arkansas were in the hands of the state's poultry and timber industries, it was argued; it was hardly a place expected to produce inspiring, principled politicians. As the New Hampshire primary loomed ahead, the Clinton campaign had a month to cloak "Slick Willie" in respectability.

Campaign director James Carville, deputy campaign manager George Stephanopoulos—and Hillary Clinton—went to work putting together a strategy. Keeping the campaign strong would mean anticipating stories before they leaked, plugging up the leaks with watertight denials, or turning them around with positive "spins" before they could turn into an avalanche of catastrophic proportions. They would repackage Bill Clinton as a good-natured, well-intentioned "Bubba" and tone down the wily aspects of the "Willie" problem. No one was more centrally involved in that repackaging than Hillary. She had given up her natural hair color, her glasses, and her maiden name to help remake the governor in his 1982 election bid—and it had worked. For the presidency, she was ready to go for broke. And at first, it seemed, going for broke wasn't really all that bad.

When the stories of Bill's marital infidelities started circulating nationwide, Hillary was quickly on the case. At her prodding, way back in September, he had faced the press—even before declaring his candidacy. It was a move reminiscent of the television ads he had purchased during his two years of disgraced banishment from the Arkansas governor's mansion when, before he had even declared he would run again, he

had apologized to the state's voters for the errors he
agreed he had made during his first tenure in office.
Bill Clinton had learned some lessons from that experience ten year earlier, and he had also paid close heed
to the errors of Gary Hart. Polls had shown that 39 percent of the voters would have reservations about voting
for a candidate who had been unfaithful to his wife.
They further stated that that number would diminish
considerably if the wife knew about the infidelity and
had accepted it.

So, at a Washington breakfast with reporters that
fall, with Hillary at his side, Bill had admitted that his
marriage hadn't been perfect. He and Hillary had
worked hard to stay together, he said, and they were
proud of their union.

"We are committed to our marriage and its obligations, to our child and to each other. We love each
other very much," he said. "Like nearly anybody
that's been together twenty years, our relationship has
not been perfect or free of difficulties. But we feel good
about where we are. We believe in our obligations. And
we intend to be together thirty or forty years from
now, regardless of whether I run for president or not."

After a pause, he concluded, "And I think that
ought to be enough."

It all worked. Having survived the grueling scrutiny
of Washington's top journalists, including David
Broder, Robert Novak, Morton Kondracke, Fred
Barnes, and Eleanor Clift, Clinton was crowned "Most
Electable" by the national press. Hillary was recognized too. At the end of the breakfast meeting, just
before she left to return to Little Rock, where Chelsea
had a school open house, reporters asked her if she
herself would make a good candidate for president.
They then asked Bill for comment.

"If she would run," he said, "I would gladly withdraw." Having her at his side would thereafter prove indispensable.

As the campaign year began, Hillary became a star in her own right. She was beautiful, articulate, and politically savvy—"far better organized, more in control, more intelligent and more eloquent," the candidate said, than was he. As things heated up, she gained strength. The worse things looked, the better did she. Standing resolutely by his side, Hillary seemed to give weight to Bill Clinton's often fragile campaign. Perhaps it was in part subliminal: if Bill Clinton could be supported, believed in—even loved—by such a formidable woman, the message was—how could the average voter not follow? Hillary was a person who would not waver, or "waffle", as the Republicans later delighted in saying about Bill Clinton. She was, many wagered, the better politician. Accordingly, in the early days the campaign gave her free rein.

"Two for the price of one!" was the offer Bill Clinton made in those early weeks. "Buy one, get one free!" he exclaimed at his fund-raisers, with Hillary close by. "If I get elected president", he said, "it will be an unprecedented partnership, far more than Franklin Roosevelt and Eleanor. They were two great people, but on different tracks. If I get elected, we'll do things together like we always have."

This was Hillary Clinton's Golden Age. Her wide smile rarely left her face, though her eyes did keep a guarded look. Commentators were struck by her ability to connect with her audience, by the way she was able to pack the full punch of her message. "Why isn't she the candidate?" some observers asked. There was talk of Hillary Clinton as a Cabinet officer, as vice president, as attorney general. She herself quickly brushed off the job of vice president: "I'm not interested in attending a lot of funerals around the world," but the suggestion of a high-level administration post did not seem entirely beyond the realm of possibility. "I want maneuverability . . ." she said. "I want to get deeply involved in solving problems." If she couldn't quite see herself in the Cabinet, Hillary did not rule out the possibility of work as an all-around adviser.

The campaign was not foolhardy, though. They knew the American public was unlikely to embrace a first lady who admitted she had her eye on a high-level administration appointment. In reality, due to the Postal Revenue and Federal Salary Act of 1967 (also called the Bobby Kennedy law, passed in response to his appointment as attorney general under John F. Kennedy) that would have been illegal). But they didn't publicize that fact very forcibly—or didn't know it. They planned to build Hillary Clinton up gradually. They planned to show her slowly to the American people, let them warm to her, and then allow them to claim her as one of their own.

But then the dam burst. At 6:30 A.M. on January 16, James Carville awoke to the sound of his phone ringing. As he reached for the receiver, he felt his stomach twist in a knot. George Stephanopoulos was on the line with bad news. He spoke rapidly, his voice shaking. He'd been given a tip: "the *Star*, a supermarket tabloid, was about to run an article alleging that Bill Clinton had had a twelve-year affair with a woman with the unlikely name of Gennifer Flowers.

The story of their affair was not new. Rumors had been circulating for so long that it seemed like old news. The gossip that the governor of Arkansas had for years been cavorting with a nightclub singer whose claim to fame had once been top billing at the Pinnacle Lounge in Little Rock (but who claimed to have made television reporting an earlier career choice) had just the edge of real-life smuttiness to play big in the supermarket scandal sheets and "feature" programs like *A Current Affair*. Until now it hadn't seemed credible enough to go prime time. The Governor had steadfastly denied the relationship, and Flowers did seem so untrustworthy a source, that the news media had not pursued the issue. Even now she was saying it was only a casual fling—though clearly had been serious enough to her to warrant the taping of phone conversations. And now the *Star* was claiming to have those tapes.

Carville dressed quickly and ran to his car. In minutes he was at National Airport, where the candidate's private plane was stopping en route to New Hampshire. The campaign staff arrived at their motel in Manchester just in time to see the *Star* story coming in over the front desk fax machine.

"MY 12-YEAR AFFAIR WITH BILL CLINTON," its front-page headline read. The staff turned their motel into a kind of makeshift dorm. Staffers doubled up in rooms and stuffed towels in the doors to keep them from locking so that any room could be opened for a meeting at any time.

Carville's first phone call was to Hillary. "How's Bill?" she asked. Her voice registered no sign of distress, he later told *Newsweek*. She grilled him, and he was grateful for the steady focus her questions gave him. This was a battle, she reassured him, that she and Bill would fight, once again, together.

His brief hopefulness swiftly fading, Carville returned to the governor. Clinton, he was annoyed to find, seemed incomprehensibly serene. In the van on the way to a campaign rally he dozed, and then lazily leafed through *Lincoln on Leadership*. Hillary, when Carville spoke with her again a few hours later, had had the time to work up a rage. She said she wanted to nip the thing in the bud, to go public. Ted Koppel had already contacted the Clinton campaign, and offered the governor time to respond to the *Star* on *Nightline*. The campaign first said yes, and then reversed itself. Respond to the *Star*? It seemed absurd. But some kind of damage control was clearly necessary. It was time to bring out the Hillary and Bill show for another round.

They faced logistical problems, however. Hillary was busy campaigning in Atlanta, and Bill was enmeshed in New Hampshire primary electioneering. There was no way they could unite to prepare and deliver a response for that night's newscast. For once the fates of press scheduling worked in their favor. The Gennifer Flowers story didn't make the evening news.

The Clintons rushed to meet. Bill got back to the governor's mansion first. It was a Friday night and he shuddered, waiting for Hillary to return, as he realized that very night, a man was being executed in an Arkansas jail. When Carolyn Staley called, he came to the phone.

"I guess we've had two executions today," she said.

When Bill answered, he spoke so softly and slowly that she had trouble understanding him. "I got to go," he said then, breaking off. "Hillary's home."

Working late into the night, they hammered out a position and worked through their respective scripts. In the end, it had all come down to a simple decision: go public or give up. One thing a Clinton candidacy could not sustain was evasiveness or half-truths, which could be read as a sign of dishonesty. Faced with a choice between minimum damage containment and an all-out frontal attack, the Clintons, hoping for a repeat performance of their September success, chose to stand and fight. The vehicle they finally agreed on was as risky as any could be: a special episode of *60 Minutes* immediately following the Super Bowl. It was a scary prospect: viewers, hyped from an afternoon of beer-swilling and TV-side cheers, would kick off their evening with a visit from the first family of Arkansas—airing the worst of their dirty laundry.

Bill Clinton was, not surprisingly, squeamish about the idea. It was one thing to go public before an audience of two hundred largely jaded journalists, leaving it to their deadpan prose to translate his feelings into newspaper inches, and quite another to discuss marriage and infidelity before the zoom lens of prime-time television. His face, he knew, tended to be very expressive, his emotions close to the surface. What guarantee was there that his eyes wouldn't cloud with feeling or that, at inopportune moments, his mouth wouldn't be caught turning down in a scowl? *60 Minutes*, unlike Larry King, could not be counted upon to provide a sympathetic sounding block for his peculiar sort of public apologies. He and Hillary would have to wing it—and put their trust in the empathetic instincts of the nation's viewers.

Hillary had some reason to think they might be. On January 18, at a campaign rally in Bedford, New Hampshire, when someone had asked her if marital fidelity should be a campaign issue, she had faced the four hundred-strong crowd, Bill by her side, and responded, "In any marriage, there are issues that come up between two people who are married that I think are their business." The crowd applauded almost half a minute. "From my perspective," she said, "our marriage is a strong marriage. We love each other, support each other, and we have had a lot of strong and important experiences together that have meant a lot to us." She was proud of her family, Hillary said, and added in conclusion that she thought that what should matter to New Hampshire residents was how their own families were doing. The barb was met with uproarious applause. Clearly the public taste for Gary Hart scandals in a recession year was less than the Republicans might have hoped for.

On January 26, in a crowded anteroom of the Clintons' suite at the Ritz-Carlton Hotel in Boston, the campaign staff stood frozen before a TV monitor as CBS reporter Steve Kroft taped his forty-five-minute interview. "I have acknowledged wrongdoing," the governor offered to the camera. "I have acknowledged causing pain in my marriage." For aides who had been with Clinton since his 1982 reelection bid for governorship, there was an eerie sense of déjà vu. Once again the boy wonder was asking Mom and Dad if he could come in from the doghouse. Would humble pie play on national TV? the aides wondered. And they asked each other, crossing their fingers and saying prayers, could a confessional Clinton remember to play by new rules?

Before the interview, the campaign had decided that Bill Clinton's only hope of not falling into an endless quagmire of questions about the history of his marriage was to refuse to speak specifically about any single alleged affair. But the governor was not a very wily interviewee.

"I am assuming from your answer that you're categorically denying that you ever had an affair with Gennifer Flowers." Kroft, aiming to force Clinton to make a specific admission, carefully set his trap.

"I've said that before," the Governor said, taking the bait. "And so has she." The tension in the anteroom was so pointed that one aide developed a migraine. Others broke into nervous, hysterical giggles. Carville, whose emotions were known to strike a pitch even higher than the candidate's, broke down and wept.

Shiftily circumspect though he can be on issues he doesn't much like to face, Clinton also has a tendency to be overly open with people, and is not generally as strong as he might be at knowing when to stop giving of himself. Therein lay a root of the history of Gennifer Flowers-type problems. The seeds of prime-time disaster were ready to bloom.

"You've said that your marriage has had problems," Kroft pressed on. "What does that mean?"

"I don't me—" Clinton stopped.

". . . you were separated?" broke in Kroft. "Does it mean adultery?"

Clinton paused again. Hillary's gaze on him was sharp and intense. After having worked together so well, for so many long years, they could almost read each other's minds.

"I think the American people, at least people who have been married for a long time, know what it means," Clinton said defiantly.

Voices rising slightly, Clinton's temper visibly shortening, he and the journalist continued their verbal volleying. Finally, Hillary broke in:

"There isn't a person watching this who would feel comfortable sitting on this couch detailing everything that ever went on in their life or their marriage," she said. "And I think it's real dangerous in this country if we don't have a zone of privacy for everybody."

Message: *That's enough.*

"I-I couldn't agree with you more," Kroft stumbled. "And I think . . . and I agree with you that everyone wants to put it behind you."

"We've gone further than anybody we know of," she said, "and that's all we're going to say."

The *60 Minutes* interview, it was generally agreed, was a success. Hillary, many said, had saved the day. Some who had witnessed the odd event went so far as to say it was Hillary's day.

She had stared at Bill as he spoke during the interview, not with the vulture-eyed glare of a Nancy Reagan (or even a slowly raging Barbara Bush), but rather with a rapt attention that conveyed a sort of indulgence. If Bill didn't make his point clearly enough, Hillary slipped in. When Bill seemed poised to waffle, Hillary cut him off. "She was in control," Steve Kroft later told *Vanity Fair*. "Hillary is tougher and more disciplined than Bill is," he said. "And she's analytical. Among his faults, he has a tendency not to think of the consequences of things he says. I think she knows. She's got a ten-second delay. If something comes to her mind she doesn't think will play right, she cuts it off before anybody knows she's thinking it."

The *60 Minutes* crew had arrived in Boston the night before the broadcast to set up their equipment in the Clintons' suite. Kroft was struck then by the unflinching élan of the candidate's wife, who was scheduled to announce to the nation on Super Bowl Sunday that the man she loved was an adulterer. She busily quizzed the crew on colors and camera angles. If she was agitated, he said, it didn't show. "We fiddled around with who should sit on which side, and they fiddled around with chair heights and things like that," he said. "If you didn't know she was his wife, you'd have thought she was a media consultant. She didn't do it in a dictatorial sort of way. . . . She was very delightful and charming. When she left the room, everyone pretty much said, 'Boy, she's terrific' "

One moving scene that did not get much press occurred moments before the crew started filming. A row of lights held high on a pipe crashed to the floor, just missing Hillary's head. She jumped out of the way into Bill's arms, and they embraced for about thirty seconds. Then she straightened up and went on with the interview.

Hillary came so close to dominating the *60 Minutes* interview that the CBS team found themselves rationing her sound bites to keep her from burying Bill. Yet despite the careful editing, Hillary nonetheless emerged as the more articulate, the more forcefully secure Clinton. She had, incontestably, made the *60 Minutes* appearance a success. In the popular eye, the word of a graciously groomed married woman carries much more weight than that of a sleazily clad, cheaply made-up nightclub singer. Daunting as she was as a lawyer and campaigner, Hillary also proved that, as a wife, she was a force to be reckoned with. Soon she was to be an even more dominant figure in Bill Clinton's campaign.

Disaster, however, was just around the bend. As Gail Sheehy observed on the campaign trail, it all happened like this: In Pierre, South Dakota, on Monday, January 27, Hillary Clinton turned on CNN for her mid-morning news fix—and froze. Gennifer Flowers was back, with an accompanying soundtrack of tapes featuring her and Governor Clinton. The screen swam momentarily before Hillary's eyes. This was terrible. She waited for a moment, composed herself, then turned to her staff.

"Let's get Bill on the phone," she calmly ordered her campaign manager, Richard Mintz, averting her gaze from his tear-filled eyes.

"Hillary," Bill began a few minutes later, "who's going to believe this woman? Everybody knows you can be paid to do anything."

"Everybody doesn't know that," she answered, impatience mounting in her voice. They had been down this road before. "Bill, people who don't know you are going to say, 'Why were you even talking to this person?'"

The point was well taken. But they had no time to talk strategy. Hillary had a six o'clock date at a Pork Producers Rib Feed in Pierre. Shaking hands with slightly more than her usual vigor, thanking God that this small crowd of well-wishers wasn't home for the evening news, she stiffened visibly when Mintz came up and whispered in her ear: "All three nets led with the Flowers press conference." Gritting her teeth in a smile, Hillary excused herself and retreated. She ran to the one pay phone in the hall, a camera crew from *Prime Time Live* at her heels. Mintz begged them not to spotlight her.

"I promise I'll give you a shot of her on the phone, but this is not the time," he said.

As she cradled the telephone, her face suddenly fell. Her eyelids closed momentarily. In Little Rock, word was that a young woman had been offered a half million dollars to say she'd had a one-night stand with Bill Clinton. "My God," she thought. "What next?"

She turned her back to the camera crew, to Mintz, and to a few curious locals behind her. This is what campaigning is all about these days, she told herself. This was why Bill had chosen not to run for president five years earlier. This is why they had held out until they were strong, had waited for Chelsea to grow up a bit more so that she, at least, might be able to tell the difference between truth and trumped-up political lies. Hillary had to find a way out of this. She had to keep the ship afloat.

Back in the relative privacy of her six-seat charter plane, she began to sound off. "If we'd been in front of a jury, I'd say, 'Miss Flowers, isn't it true you were asked this by the A.P. in June of 1990 and you said no? Weren't you asked by the *Arkansas Democrat* and you said no? I would crucify her." The lawyerly talk was like a mantra. Hillary was returning to form, recalling her strengths. Though she talked into the tape recorder of a reporter then trailing her for an interview, her words were clearly not aimed for anyone else's ears. The reporter was only a sounding board. Hillary would talk until landing, at which time she had to have a plan.

"I'm not just going to sit by anymore and say, 'Well, it's the press's responsibility,' " she went on. "If we can destroy people with paid stories, what's next? . . . I don't think Bill appreciates how TV really doesn't give the other side. It's like negative advertising." She paused.

"A light bulb switched on behind her eyes" is how the reporter, Gail Sheehy, later described it. Hillary's legally trained mind was warming to the fight.

"That's what I should have told him. In 1980 the Republicans started the negative advertising; in 1992 we have paid political character assassination." Her words slowed a little as she let her thoughts unfold. "What Bill doesn't understand is you've gotta do the same thing in response as you do with negative advertising—Dukakis didn't understand that." Excited, she picked up the pace: "This is the daughter of Willie Horton!"

Rapid City, Iowa, loomed ahead. The airstrip below was an endless field of blackness. A lone sign, mounted on a flimsy shack, announced the city's presence. For the less hardy aides on the plane, it was impossible not to think of the end of the world.

Hillary barely stayed seated for the plane's bumpy landing. The minute the cabin door opened, she was out the door, clicking down the concrete landing strip in her high heels, mentally rehearsing the conference call she would soon hold with her husband and the campaign staff.

She had a new strategy all mapped out. Make the "Republican attack machine" the villain in this scandal, Hillary said, don't let Bill Clinton's "character issues" steal the headlines. The press, favored target of

Republicans and Democrats alike, could take more than its share of the blame. Hillary clicked off priorities. "Who's getting information on the *Star*? Who's tracking down the research on Gennifer? Where is our surrogate program? Who's going to be out there speaking for us?"

The blanched faces of her younger staffers made her pause. She and Bill would be out there on the front lines fighting, she assured them. "But I want you to be putting this stuff together."

Months later, George Stephanopoulos would retain the memory of this night. "It was inspirational," he told Sheehy.

James Carville approved of Hillary's advice—and took it one step further. When the *60 Minutes* episode aired and he saw that the Governor had only received nine of the fifteen-to-eighteen minutes of airtime CBS had promised, he refused to make the best of a bad situation. CBS, he publicly stated, had "screwed" Clinton. They had edited out his best moments—for example, when he explained why he wanted to be president. Thus began a short-lived crusade against the press. Carville soon was denouncing every reporter he saw as a "cash for trash" journalist. At a New Jersey fund-raiser, surrounded by reporters and TV cameras, he ranted so much that after about five minutes a confused rookie interrupted to ask if he was in fact with the Clinton campaign. "Yes," Carville retorted, "and I'm a lot more expensive than Gennifer Flowers."

It turned out that Flowers *had* been paid—$50,000, Bill Clinton said; $130,000 or $170,000, Hillary asserted. And there were many more interesting details than that. The *Star* story was actually based upon a lawsuit filed in 1990 by Larry Nichols, a former employee of the Arkansas Development Finance Agency, who had been fired by the state for making at least 142 long-distance fund-raising calls from his office on behalf of the Nicaraguan contras, running up a huge telephone bill at taxpayer expense. Rather than filing a grievance, he began collecting Clinton gossip and waiting to take revenge. His opportunity came in the fall of 1990, during Clinton's ugly reelection race against Sheffield Nelson. Nichols sent Clinton several cagey letters alluding to knowledge of sexual misconduct. When Clinton ignored them, Nichols sued, alleging that he had been fired as part of a cover-up of a slush fund used to finance Clinton's adulterous adventures. He tried to subpoena five women, including a few beauty queens, a Clinton aide, and Flowers for depositions. He told a journalist that he had tapes on which the women discussed their affairs with Clinton, but never produced them. He kept announcing the time and place where the women would be deposed, but no one ever appeared. Nichols then turned to the Republicans. He reportedly lunched with Robert Leslie, a Republican national committee member from Arkansas, and is said to have made contact with Republicans on Capitol Hill and in the RNC seeking financial help for his suit but was turned down.

Reports are somewhat contradictory about the exact nature of the relationship between Nelson and Nichols that fall. Nichols has said that Nelson summoned him to his office and asked him not to push the suit because he would be blamed for it. Another well-connected Arkansas Republican said, however, that Nelson had taken a public "high road" posture while spreading the stories about Clinton in private. Nelson's press secretary, John Hudges, was a friend of Flowers's, having once worked with her at a Little Rock television station. He said she had spoken about her relationship with Clinton as early as 1977. Finally, to the shock and dismay of the Nelson camp, the local news media in

Arkansas decided that Nichols's charges were slander-
ous and wrote nothing about them. Two days before
the election, according to the *Washington Post*, Nichols
called Mike Gauldin, Clinton's press secretary, and
asked to meet him at a local truck stop. Gauldin said
Nichols offered to drop his suit in exchange for a house
and $150,000, but Gauldin refused.

By the time the national press descended on Little
Rock in the summer of 1991 to check out the rumors,
they had grown to include a story that Clinton had fa-
thered an illegitimate child during the 1980s. No reliable source was ever found to back up that charge,
and all the women who were named in the suit denied
their affairs.

In January 1992, however, Stephen Edwards, a reporter for the *Star*, arrived in Little Rock. He visited a
restaurant where Flowers had been the featured singer
and asked the bartender, "Anyone here know Gennifer Flowers?" The bartender pointed at John Hudges,
who happened to be sitting nearby. The *Star* agreed to
pay her a considerable amount of money for her tapes
and her statement that she had been Clinton's lover for
twelve years. The *Star* shortly thereafter published a
rehash of the Nichols lawsuit. In the story, Flowers
claimed she had begun to see Clinton in 1977 and continued an affair with him even after she moved to Dal-
las in the early 1980s. She had told friends then about
special visits from a "Bill" from Arkansas, though
there was no evidence that "Bill" was indeed Clinton.

The Clinton campaign aggressively sought to
counter the charges, often through ridicule.

"The *Star* says Martians walk on the Earth and people have cow's heads," Bill Clinton said in New Hampshire. "It's a totally bogus lawsuit. This guy was fired
for making illegal phone calls and tried to bribe me into
giving him money, and I just wouldn't do it."

Hillary equated the story with "a conversation with Elvis." Speaking with Sam Donaldson on *Prime Time Live*, she said, "We know that this woman has admitted that the Republicans offered her money to change her story and implicate my husband after having denied it repeatedly. And we know that the former Republican gubernatorial opponent has been out beating the bushes trying to stir this up for as long as he could since he was defeated. . . . If somebody's willing to pay you $130,000 or $170,000 to say something and you get your fifteen minutes of fame and you get your picture on the front page of every newspaper and you're some failed cabaret singer who doesn't even have much of a resumé to fall back on, and what's there she lied about, you know—that's the daughter of Willie Horton, as far as I'm concerned."

Even John Robert Starr, the man who created the epithet "Slick Willie," told reporters that there was "no substance whatsoever to the charges" against Clinton and added that Nichols was "not a credible fellow. . . . He had no evidence, nothing, except he heard the same rumors the rest of us have heard."

In a move that only reinforced the campaign's view that Gennifer Flowers was a fake smoking gun for hire, she eventually gave an in-depth—and illustrated—interview to *Penthouse* magazine.

Whether in response to revelations that the *Star* had paid Flowers, or due to Carville's quite impressive histrionics, the media began to cool to the Clinton-Flowers connection. Flowers—and the *Star*—were too easily discredited. There was, however, one last notable news conference in which Flowers, standing alongside a blow-up of the *Star* story, said Clinton's denials of their affair had hurt her deeply. The crowd of reporters showed little pity. The conference deteriorated rather rapidly.

"Did the governor use a condom?" one reporter shouted, while the others hooted with laughter. They laughed even harder when Blake Hendrick, Gennifer Flowers's attorney, threatened to end the news conference "if there are any further questions that are degrading in my opinion."

Flowers did attest that a local Republican had approached her six months earlier to ask if she would publicly admit to an affair.

The media was then waking up to the fact that it had made a fool of itself. It soon came to light that one of the sources of the infidelity stories was a local food vendor named Robert "Say" McIntosh, a political gadfly who sold sweet potato pie from a truck and handed out rather lurid handbills on the streets of Little Rock accusing Clinton of extramarital affairs. McIntosh had frequently been heard to say that he was willing to spread his allegations if someone would pay his expenses.

In an effort at self-redemption, *Newsweek* then reported a series of six inconsistencies in Gennifer Flowers's story. Included was the fact that she had said she had worked on the TV show *Hee Haw* (but had not), and had stated that her first meeting with Clinton took place at the Excelsior Hotel in 1979 or 1980 (at least two years before it opened). The *New York Post*, having learned that Flowers had tape-recorded other lovers, ran a front-page story headlined, "SHE'S DONE IT BEFORE."

Clinton's favorable ratings had by now risen to 67 percent, and his negatives hung in the low 20s. The campaign heaved a sigh of relief.

The campaign's all-out frontal attack, the tactic Hillary had come to see as indispensable in the early 1980s, had saved Bill's candidacy. Her aggressive defense of him, everyone agreed, had been their best weapon of all. The problem was that in the process she had sacrificed herself.

Shortly after Hillary's impressive appearance on *60 Minutes*, a virulent backlash began. In the brief period when the attacks on Bill Clinton receded, a new "attack machine" cranked its gears into place. This time the rocks flew not at Bill's head but at Hillary's.

The exact nature of the anti-Hillary backlash is complex and multifaceted, and merits a chapter of its own. What happened in the dramatic months from January to July is, by contrast, quite straightforward.

By the first week of February, Bill Clinton was already fielding questions from reporters who sought to know if he was concerned about being upstaged by his wife. The questions didn't put him off at all. "I've always liked strong women," he said at a February 7 rally. "It doesn't bother me for people to see her and get excited and say she could be president too."

Richard Nixon, however, gave the Clintons quite a different spin. Observing the couple's progress as "co-candidates" in February, he pithily observed that a strong wife "makes the husband look like a wimp." "Hillary pounds on the piano so hard that Bill can't be heard," he said. "You want a wife who's intelligent, but not too intelligent."

Other men in the media soon seemed to feel the same way. Hillary was beginning to ruffle feathers. A normally expressionless Tom Brokaw, looking at the South for Super Tuesday, expressed shock when, at a rally after the votes came in, Hillary victoriously rushed past her husband, rose to the podium, and grabbed the microphone first. While Bill hopped up and down in the wings, she slowly worked her way through an introduction in which she referred rather sparingly to her husband—and then only as "the messenger." She concluded, "We believe passionately in this country and we cannot stand by for one more year and watch what is happening to it!" After her windup minutes later, Brokaw observed, over the din of audience applause, "Not just an introduction, this is a speech by Mrs. Clinton."

After Clinton's victory in the Illinois primary, the networks switched to campaign headquarters for a reaction from the candidate and tuned into the same scene: Hillary delivering a long and proud introduction, while Bill lingered eagerly in the back. "Like a hanger-on hungering for home-baked cookies," as William Safire described it. Brokaw and Peter Jennings once again seemed miffed. Safire accused Hillary of "usurpation of a candidate's strength."

He had written on the female-usurpation theme before. He had similarly attacked Nancy Reagan in 1987, saying that because of her "interference," Ronald Reagan was being "weakened and made to appear wimpish and helpless." Then, as in 1992, his words would have a damaging impact.

Accordingly, by late March public opinion of the candidate's overachieving wife was starting to turn. The 65 percent approval rating she had garnered earlier in the month was swiftly falling. The same thing that her friends said—that Hillary was "tougher" than Bill—was now being used against her. Even her headband was seen as the sign of a malevolent force.

"There's something a little scary, a little Al Haig-ish about her," a close observer was quoted as saying in *Vanity Fair*.

If the mainstream press was having trouble with Hillary's untraditional ways, the journalists of the right were in the throes of an all-out war. A sympathetic article by Garry Wills in the *New York Review of Books*, which detailed Hillary's legal writings and speeches from many years earlier, provoked a tidal wave of right-wing outrage. William F. Buckley's *National Review* featured a cover with a photo of Clinton captioned: "STOP—OR MY WIFE WILL SHOOT." The *American Spectator*, in an article entitled "THE LADY MACBETH OF LITTLE ROCK," compared Hillary to Eva Peron and called her the "Winnie Mandela of American politics." The article tore apart her legal theories, said she endorsed the right of children to sue parents "to solve family arguments," and accused her of having channeled illegal financial support to an assortment of left-wing causes while acting as the head of federally funded agencies. Soon a widely circulated right-wing fund-raising letter was calling Hillary "a radical feminist who has little use for religious values or even the traditional family unit."

More bad news was on the way. In March, a story surfaced that in 1978 Hillary and Bill had invested in an Ozark vacation property deal with a friend, James B. McDougal, who went on to become a Clinton administration appointee—and also the owner of an Arkansas savings and loan institution. That institution, which at some points subsidized the real estate venture, later failed—and was represented by Hillary Clinton and her Rose Law Firm when it became subject to state regulation. Hillary quickly acknowledged that she had done legal work for the savings and loan, Madison Guaranty, but stressed that it had not been related to the S&L's dealings with state regulators. She stated, furthermore, that she had refused to accept her share of earnings from any state business the Rose Law Firm might have earned since 1978, when Bill first attained statewide office.

Outside a Chicago diner, she told reporters, "I have done everything I knew how to do to be as careful as possible, including turning my back on funds that were coming into my firm." It turned out that the Clintons had improperly deducted at least $5,000 on their personal tax returns in 1984 and 1985 for interest paid on a portion of at least $30,000 in bank loan payments that the real estate company, Whitewater Development, made for them. The deductions saved them about $1,000 in taxes, but since the error was made more than three years ago, the IRS did not require the Clintons to pay. Lawyers for the Clintons said these were honest errors, made due to confusion over who really owned a certain piece of Whitewater property and who was responsible for the loan taken out to buy it.

Many other questions could not be answered, because Whitewater's records could not be located. McDougal said that at the Governor's request they had been delivered to the mansion years earlier. The Clintons said many of them had simply disappeared.

No evidence of wrongdoing ever emerged. Federal regulators finally took the savings and loan away from McDougal, and a federal grand jury charged him with fraud, though he was later acquitted. Around this time he was also found to be suffering from manic-depressive illness, though he was judged competent to stand trial. The story, which was just a bit too obtuse to make tabloid headlines, might easily have been forgotten if not for former California governor Jerry Brown's suggestion that Hillary and Bill's business connections were tantamount to "corruption." Hillary counter-attacked by charging Brown with striking a blow at all struggling two-career couples, and attributed his remarks to "pathetic and desperate" mud-slinging.

"You've got to remember", she said on a campaign stop in a Chicago bakery, "that I have tried the best way I know how to be as careful as possible. Now, in hindsight, I suppose people can say, 'You should have done this, you should have done that.' I didn't presume that anybody would presume anything other than that I was trying to do the right thing all the way down the line."

Then she made the comment that would haunt her for the rest of the campaign: "I suppose I could have stayed home and baked cookies and had teas," she said. "But what I decided to do was pursue my profession, which I entered before my husband was in public life."

She was clearly enraged. She had taken particular offense at an offhand remark Brown had made that she felt was an insult to her as a working wife. "In response to a question about his father's law firm doing business with the state when he was governor, he said, 'Well, I don't control my father,' " Hillary commented on the *Today* show. "And you know, it wasn't very subtle, and I was trying to point out that his attitude seemed to be that I should have only confined myself to the ceremonial role of a first lady."

Barbara Bush clearly appreciated her anger, and spoke out against Brown's attack and in favor of Hillary Clinton's right to a career. But the public did not prove receptive to Hillary's outrage.

A surprisingly wide portion of the public cried foul. Hillary had already, on *60 Minutes*, offended people with her line, "I'm not some little woman standing by her man like Tammy Wynette." For that she had had to issue an official apology, after Wynette had sent her a letter that read, "Mrs. Clinton, you have offended every woman and man who love that song—several million in number. I believe you have offended every true country music fan and every person who has 'made it on their own' with no one to take them to a White House."

Hillary's unapologetic intelligence, her combativeness, her refusal to do anything other than speak her mind, had been wearing on the nerves of America's change-wary voters for some weeks now. The "cookies and tea" comment was just too much. Hillary had crossed a line that was, to many, still sacred. Millions of women who had never worked outside the home read Hillary's statement as a contemptuous insult. Overnight, their indignation inflamed by the press, they turned on her.

The Arkansas Travelers, friends of Bill and Hillary's who helped out on the campaign trail, encountered voters who said they wouldn't vote for Bill Clinton because they baked cookies, because their daughters baked cookies, because they were "afraid" of Hillary. "I feel like she's the power behind the throne." "I think she's a very aggressive woman, and she's overly ambitious." "She has no use for us, we have no use for her," average Americans were quoted saying in April.

One week after the infamous "cookie" line, William Safire coined the phrase the "Hillary Problem." In an op-ed piece published in the March 26 *New York Times*, he accused her of "elitism in action," and attributed her two major gaffes—the "cookie" line and her politically incorrect sneer at Tammy Wynette—to a severe case of "foot-in-mouth disease." Using the very sort of self-help jargon he loved to hate, he proposed a "six-step solution" to the problem of Hillary, which suggested, among its more salient features, that she be banished from taking the podium for victory statements or concession speeches.

Such censure came as a shock to her. As a lawyer, she was so used to choosing her words carefully that to have been caught in a blooper truly came as a blow. She insisted her words had been taken out of context. They'd become, she said, a "misconstruction." Her choice of phrase, which once again lacked just the warmth and softness she needed, was hard as armor, and its unconscious brittleness betrayed the fact that she had been truly hurt. When asked a few weeks later about the gaffe, she gave, uncharacteristically, a somewhat halting response. "I don't know how to feel about it. . . . I think I'll just have to be more careful in the way I express my feelings, so I don't inadvertently hurt anybody," she told Gail Sheehy. "I can understand why some people thought that I was criticizing women who made different choices from the ones I had—in fact, criticizing the choice that my mother and a lot of dear friends have made. Nothing could be further from what I believe."

The media was not about to let a situation rife with such inflammatory possibilities die. Throughout March, Hillary made headlines and cover stories. Soon it seemed that the more column inches were devoted to the "Hillary Problem," the greater that problem became. The *New York Times*, for example, ran an article that prominently quoted the views of two elderly, anti-Hillary work-at-homebodies. Having resolved among themselves whether to identify themselves as "retired homemakers" or "housewives" by settling upon the latter term ("Is that word O.K. by Hillary?"), they opined that she was up to no good.

"She's only interested in being with a winner," seventy-one-year-old Bernadine Elliott said. "And believe me, if he doesn't get elected, she's going to dump him. Mark my words."

"That's right. She'll dump him," sixty-nine-year-old LaRoux Tanner agreed. Although dozens of other voters interviewed for the article voiced positive views of Hillary, the Elliott quote was the one picked up and repeated in the weekly news magazines.

There were additional ethics charges too. In late March, the *Times* reported that Bill Clinton had supported an ethics and disclosure law for public officials, but with his advisers had altered it before it was approved by voters in 1988 so that he and other public officials were exempt from disclosing potential conflicts of interest, such as questions related to state dealings with the Rose Law Firm. The deletion occurred during a private drafting session, with participants including Clinton, close political aides, allies, and Webb Hubbell, a senior partner at Rose, the *Times* said, though Clinton and Hubbell denied it.

Hillary, understandably, was growing bitter—and the tension was starting to show. Her image was not improved when, in an article to be published in the May issue of *Vanity Fair*, she complained to Gail Sheehy about the "double standard" in the press, which had focused so much on her husband's infidelities and ignored a long-rumored, long-term affair between George Bush and Jennifer Fitzgerald, a loyal staffer now employed in a senior position in the state department. Referring to a conversation she had held with Anne Cox Chambers, the chairwoman of Cox newspapers, Hillary said: "She's sittin' there in her sunroom saying, 'You know, I just don't understand why they think they can get away with this—everybody knows about George Bush's carrying on, all of which is apparently well-known in Washington."

By referring to George Bush's purported affair, Hillary dared what no Washington reporter had ever put in print. Once again she had crossed a sacred line. The newspapers were quick to castigate her, their glee barely contained behind shocked banner headlines: "HILLARY'S REVENGE," "HILLARY GOES TABLOID," and "BILL'S WIFE DISHES THE DIRT." Even Barbara Bush was moved to make a public statement of outrage.

Hillary had no choice but to backpedal—fast. This occurred three days before New York's Democratic primary, and the Clinton campaign could ill afford scandal in a then lukewarm state. Borrowing a technique from the Bush campaign—attack and "repent"—on April 4, Hillary apologized. Campaigning for her husband at the College of St. Rose in Albany, she said, "It was a mistake. People were asking me questions at the time and I responded, but nobody knows better than I the pain that can be caused by discussing rumors in private conversation."

Bush's "Jennifer" did not make as much of a splash as the Clinton campaign had probably hoped. But the accusation—a poor strategic move on Hillary's part—did help drive another nail into the coffin of her good standing. The idea had promise: Hillary would make the accusation, Bill would be guilt-free, and if Bush retaliated, the campaign would be able to call his attacks mere attempts at saving face. But it didn't work. The comment merely sank Hillary lower in public opinion. Voters, she was quickly learning, hear what they want to hear. George Bush was not about to be smeared by the accusations of his opponent's wife.

In the popular mind, Hillary's name was quick becoming a buzzword for everything that was a bit too cold, a bit too opportunistic, a bit too mean about successful working women. One cartoon in the *New Yorker* showed a woman asking a salesclerk for a jacket and saying, "Nothing too Hillary."

New York primary polls found Hillary Clinton's approval rating down to around 35 percent. While a minority still said they found her strong and inspirational, the overwhelming majority now seemed to have swung over to the Richard Nixon school of gender relations. More and more, voters who otherwise admired the candidate's wife's strength and candor now worried that she overwhelmed her husband. "What does it tell you about a Presidential candidate if people say:

'His wife will back him up. His wife will run the White House?' " one voter rhetorically asked in the *New York Times*. "I want the President to be President."

After the New York primary, Hillary retreated from the national stage. She would emerge again in late spring fully rehabilitated as the picture-perfect caring wife and doting mother. The line from the Clinton campaign was that Hillary wouldn't have any special influence in the White House, and that she herself would insist upon taking only an unpaid job. Her campaign appearances now combined still passionate speechmaking with Donna Reed-like poses. Hillary cut ribbons at openings of new campaign headquarters and read stories like "Chicka Chicka Boom Boom" to children in preschool classes, against a backdrop of plastic ironing boards and stoves. She let a bit of an Arkansas twang creep into her voice, talked much about Chelsea and her interest in education. Her photo opportunities were designed to have her surrounded by small children. She would look warm and maternal, and her headband now seemed more schoolmarmish than like the velvet crown of a yuppie-from-hell.

Most important, she worked hard to reassure voters that Bill Clinton wasn't a wimp. "He has a real core of toughness," she said at one rally. She reiterated his new promise not to offer her a Cabinet post: "That's not going to happen and I wouldn't take it if it did." She swore she would not sit in on Cabinet meetings: "I never did that in Arkansas and I'm not going to start now." And she demurred on the question of becoming a radical, pioneering first lady: "I don't think so; I hope I'm going to be myself."

In a conversation with David Frost in late May, she dismissed a reference to one of her husband's earlier statements that the Clinton's reign in the White House would be an "unprecedented partnership," greater than that of the Roosevelts, as "very nice hyperbole."

She even, though somewhat disingenuously, tried to sidestep the label of "feminist" she had proudly claimed for so many years. Like Bill, she believed in equality, but now she rejected some of "what the term has come to mean today."

"I don't think feminism, as I understand the definition, implies the rejection of maternal values, nurturing children, caring about the men in your life," she said. "That is just nonsense to me."

Though Hillary wasn't about to give up the feminist mantle altogether, she wasn't flaunting it, either. Instead she began drawing comparisons of herself and Barbara Bush. "We're both very committed women. We care very deeply about our families, and we're supportive of our husbands," she said of Barbara, who identifies herself on her tax returns as a "housewife." (Hillary reportedly files under the name of Rodham.)

The effort to sustain a common link to Barbara was never clearer than when, on Memorial Day weekend, Hillary addressed the graduating class of Wellesley College. Barbara Bush had been asked to speak two years earlier, and her selection had touched off a storm of controversy on the highly feminist campus. About a fourth of the graduating class said they believed that Mrs. Bush, someone who had dropped out of college to marry, was a poor choice, and had only been invited because of her husband.

In accordance with her new "kinder, gentler" image, Hillary made a point of praising women who decide to stay at home to raise families as well as those who choose careers. "You may choose to be a corporate executive or a rocket scientist, you may run for public office, or you may stay home and raise your children," she said. "You can now make any or all of these choices, and they can be the work of your life." She delivered a pointed attack on Dan Quayle's "family values" crusade: "Women who pack lunches for their kids or take the early bus to work, or stay out late at the P.T.A. or spend every minute tending to their aging parents, do not need lectures from Washington about values. They don't need to hear about an idealized world that never was as righteous or as carefree as some would like to think." But she also made sure to add that her daughter, Chelsea, "has been the joy of our life."

She told graduates that she had made her life's work helping children and said that in their future lives there would be many ways to do so too. "You can do it by making policy or by making cookies," she said to applause.

Walking the fine line between feminist and the Democratic version of "family values," Hillary entered July with a damagingly low approval rating of 29 percent. The Democratic National Convention was approaching; it was time for even more serious action. Hillary, at long last, ascended to the ranks of sound-bite first ladydom. At an appearance in a high school in Conway, Arkansas, a student asked her what her role in the Clinton administration would be. Hillary lowered her voice, ladylike, to answer. "I want to be the voice for children in the White House," she said softly. It was "Just Say No" fine-tuned to perfection. Then she went even further. In June, on the day of the California primary, she had been taken hostage by her good friends Mary Steenburgen and Linda Bloodworth-Thomason, who brought her three top production stylists—Christophe for hair, Charlie Blackwell for makeup, Cliff Chally for wardrobe—along with a trio of salespeople from Ron Ross, a Studio City designer boutique. Hillary spent the day in a bathrobe, trying on clothes. The result was that Christophe cut five inches off her hair and recolored it "honey blonde," and Hillary showed up in Madison Square Garden with a newly revitalized, more glamorous wardrobe. The night of Bill Clinton's acceptance speech at Madison Square Garden, she wore a pastel yellow silk suit. She even grabbed Tipper Gore by the wrist and led her in a dance, looking "like 1960s teenyboppers recovering their lost youth," as Bill so aptly describe to *W*.

Chelsea was pulled out of privacy and marched around to prove to the doubting public that the Clintons did, in fact, have a child. Swallowing her distaste, Hillary allowed *People* magazine to run a profile of Chelsea (without her daughter's participation) and shared opinions for the story on issues ranging from ear-piercing to questions on the facts of life.

Child rearing, dessert recipes, and the Fourth of July became Hillary's topics of the day. She tolerated reporters' queries on her clothes. She wore pastels. She made news in the days before the convention by promoting her chocolate chip cookie recipe in a reader's choice cookie bake-off between herself and Barbara Bush. The competition was sponsored by *Family Circle* magazine, which had seized the opportunity provided by Hillary's unfortunate cookie comment to combine a recipe feature with timely current events.

"I want to have fun," she was heard saying on her first day in New York City. "I want to win the cookie bake-off."

In the days before the convention, with an energy and enthusiasm attributable only to a colossal act of sublimation, Hillary promoted her recipe for chocolate chip cookies. On Monday, she told an audience of congressional wives at a tea given in her honor that although she wasn't accustomed to being competitive (not her!), she was going to win.

"Join with me in the first real effort of the election year," she implored her supporters. "Try my cookies. I hope you like them, but like good Democrats vote for them anyway." Whether Hillary actually took the time to bake a batch of her cookies for the convention-time bake-off is unclear. The cookies at the tea were baked by Powell Weeks, a cook who works for one of Mrs. Clinton's friends, Norma Asnes. Other friends from around the country baked cookies too, and would, in a uniquely feminine show of support for Hillary, have passed them out on the floor of Madison Square Garden had not the Garden's management ruled that health regulations made doing so illegal. At the last minute the Soutine Bakery was hired to deliver six thousand cookies.

In what was undoubtedly one of the silliest moments in Hillary's campaign, she appeared cum recipe, in an article in the *New York Times*'s Living section. Her quotes, in the newspaper's former ladies page, were appropriately pithy: "My friends say my recipe is more democratic," she boasted, "because I use vegetable shortening instead of butter." Hillary's cookies, made with oatmeal and vegetable shortening, were deemed more politically correct—and lower in calories too—than Barbara Bush's butter-laden ones, according to food writer Marion Burros. The article was capped with a picture of Hillary and Tipper Gore taking time out from their busy cookie campaign to have tea at the Waldorf.

In the heat of the Democratic National Convention, Hillary Clinton's new act was not convincing. Her wide-eyed, down-home comments were so extraordinarily hokey that they sounded almost intentionally fake. "I almost have to pinch myself to believe I am going to New York to see my husband nominated for the presidency of the United States," was a prize one—

"corny as Kansas in August," as one newspaper reporter described her.

"I am an old-fashioned patriot. I cry at the Fourth of July when kids put crepe paper on their bicycle wheels, so this is, like, just incredible, it's so extraordinary to me," she purred on. Her evolution pleased no one. *New York Times* reporter Joyce Purnick, in an editorial, begged the convention to "LET HILLARY BE HILLARY," while Republican consultant Roger Ailes commented, "Hillary Clinton in an apron is like Michael Dukakis in a tank."

The *Arkansas Democrat-Gazette*'s intelligently vituperative Paul Greenberg told *W* that the transformation had worked to Hillary's disadvantage. "The first time I saw Hillary Rodham, she was angry about injustice and not fearful or calculating about saying so. She was more ideologically committed, less fashionably attractive. Now she's tough, controlled, cosmetologized, intense, with something contradictory under the surface. You have the idea she's holding back."

The least victorious person to emerge after the jubilant Democratic convention was, perhaps, Hillary Clinton. Seven months of running for cover on the political battlefield had taken their toll. Hillary wasn't, of course, the candidate; she hadn't been judged for her political platform. Only her self that had been in the line of fire—her personality, her integrity, her marriage. Even the most resilient person would have cracked a bit under those circumstances. Hillary wasn't the type, though, to cry on friends' shoulders.

The one moment she broke down a bit during the campaign had come when she'd shared sympathy with a friend over the press's treatment of her marriage—and then it was Hillary who ended up giving the dry-eyed comfort. This had been during the hellish month of January, the time of Gennifer Flowers. Hillary phoned her close friend and confidante Carolyn Huber. Huber broke into sobs. In an unusually soft and wavering voice, Hillary comforted her. Uncharacteristically, she admitted her own pain. "It's hurting so bad, Carolyn," she said, according to Huber's account in *Vanity Fair*. "The press doesn't believe you have any feelings. They sure don't believe in the Bible."

Having brought Bill Clinton "back from the dead," as he describes it, what life was left in Hillary? After the Democratic Convention, *Newsweek*'s Eleanor Clift compared the wifely Hillary of July to the lion of the past winter and said, "Today's Hillary is a burned-out, buttoned-up automaton compared with the vibrant woman who strode purposefully onto the national scene last January." The statement was cruel in its starkness, but it did point out a very real change in Hillary's demeanor. She has always been known to have a brittle, almost nasty side. It's a side that emerges only when she's angry, or hurt, and often takes the form of pointed irony.

This had emerged early on in the campaign year. In New Hampshire, she had quickly realized that the celebrity the Clintons were achieving had an ugly side. She had made that point clear to the staff one day when, with Clinton's approval rating plummeting in the polls after the first draft and infidelity fiascoes, a surprisingly large number of people showed up to see him in Nashua. An aide happily suggested that the polls had been wrong. Why else would so many people show up to cheer Clinton on a cold New England day? In a voice meant to end conversation, Hillary answered: "You don't know why they're here. They may just want to see the freak show," she told *Newsweek*.

Hillary's three transformations—from wounded wife to campaign crusader to perfect political wife—

took their toll. Her battering by the press had, too. She summed up her feelings about its treatment of her during the campaign with a simple nursery rhyme: "As I was standing in the street as quiet as can be/A great big ugly man came up and tied his horse to me." Or, as she put it to the editors of the Grand Junction, Colorado, *Daily Sentinel*: "You feel like you're standing in the middle of a firing range, and sometimes they come close to hitting you on the top of the head."

By summer Hillary no longer believed that the media could help her convey the truth about her marriage or her political views. The cookies business had all been a scam: *Family Circle* had asked her for a recipe without telling her it was to be used in a bake-off against Barbara Bush. Mrs. Bush hadn't even been given a fighting chance; her recipe had been reprinted from a 1986 article in *McCall's*. Hillary's cookie lobbying at the time of the convention had been purposefully tongue-and-cheek, but the press had treated it as seriously as a policy statement. Her substantive statements, her appearances before a pro-Israel lobby and her meeting with the nation's highest-ranking women politicians, went largely unnoticed. She was tired of having her hair and her clothing make news. She was angry too about news stories that described her as having been "muzzled."

In truth, she had never stopped making speeches, and she had certainly never dropped out of campaign work. But the perception by the press that the nature of her public appearances had changed stuck nevertheless, and in mid-November was vindicated when, in an unusual scoop, the *New York Times* reported that in late April a confidential campaign memo from Stan Greenberg, the campaign's polling expert, chief strategist James Carville, and media consultant Frank Greer urged the Clintons to rehabilitate their image in order to appear a warmer, more simple and loving couple. The fourteen-page confidential document called "The General Election Project—Interim Report" suggested that to counter the images voters had of Hillary Clinton as "being in the race for herself," "going for the power," and being intent on "running the show," Hillary should start arranging "joint appearances with her friends where Hillary can laugh, do her mimicry," and perhaps stage an event where "Bill and Chelsea surprise Hillary on Mother's Day."

There was little comment on that document by the former campaign crew. Just a few weeks before, Hillary had stopped giving long interviews anyway. By early fall she was alloting reporters small portions of time during twenty-minute car rides to this or that event. She stopped making small talk. She made little attempt to put reporters at ease. She delivered her responses in the fewest words possible. She sidestepped personal revelations, even avoided saying "I." With odd formality, she referred to her husband as "Bill Clinton."

Hillary's self-assurance, so striking in the early days of the campaign, had taken a blow. She could not make sense of the censure she'd gotten for her few slips of tongue on the campaign trail. She'd never gotten over the fallout from her "cookies and teas" comment. It never, really, made sense to her. There is a picture hanging in the study of the governor's mansion in Little Rock: she and Bill pictured as farmer and wife in a spoof on the painting *American Gothic*. In the picture she casts a sidelong "there you go again" look at Bill. Now, would the roles be reversed? Could their marriage, their sense of themselves, stand it?

After the Democratic convention, Hillary was often seen standing on the sidelines, her smile a little wider and softer. As "designated wife," she "stood by her man," across the podium from Tipper Gore, standing by hers. She appeared on the daytime television show *Home* and fielded questions with a group of other mothers during an advice feature called "Club Mom." She also kept up her campaign speeches, without fanfare. She continued to take time out on the campaign trail for long, quiet conversations with Chelsea. She was often heard praying: "Dear Lord, be good to me. The sea is so wide and my boat is so small."

There were three months left of the race, and Bill Clinton was buoyant. But was Hillary Rodham Clinton about to sink?

The Republican convention was still to come.

7

"The Hillary Factor"

"What does *Hillary* believe?" Patrick J. Buchanan shouted as the crowd of eager delegates, smelling blood, giggled and roared.

"What does *Hillary* believe?

"*Hillary* believes that twelve-year-olds should have the right to sue their parents. And *Hillary* has compared marriage and the family as institutions to slavery and life on an Indian reservation."

The catcalls and hoots were audible.

"Well, speak for yourself, *Hillary*."

The Republican National Convention of August 1992 was a hate fest. Homosexuals, liberals, working mothers, all were the victims in a right-wing rally that, as many in the party agreed afterward, had been permitted to run amuck. No one took more hits, however, than Hillary Clinton.

That her views would be attacked was no surprise. For weeks before, at the highest levels of the Bush campaign, the anti-Hillary machinery had been warming

up. Bush campaign manager Mary Matalin had a pho-
tograph of Hillary as the Wicked Witch of the East
posted on her office wall, captioned: "I will get you,
my pretty, and your little dog too!" One week before
the convention, Republican national chairman Rich
Bond launched the first arm of the offensive with his
jibe at "that champion of the family, Hillary Clinton,
who believes that kids should be able to sue their parents, rather than helping with the chores as they were
asked to do."

By the time Pat Buchanan began his bombast, the
mere mention of Hillary Clinton's first name sent the
Republicans in the Astrodome into fits of nasty giggles. Many were wearing buttons that read "ANOTHER
COOKIE BAKER FOR BUSH."

Buchanan was not looking for laughs, though.
Deadly serious, he accused Hillary of being a "radical
feminist" who, as part of a deadly "Clinton and Clinton" administration, would bring "abortion on demand a litmus test for the Supreme Court, homosexual
rights, discrimination against religious schools [and]
women in combat units" to the nation. Clearly, in the
battle lines drawn in the cultural war for the "soul of
America," as Buchanan had previously called it, Hillary Clinton was on the side of the damned.

More shocking than Buchanan's prime-time political
rhetoric, however, were the off-camera attacks on Hillary, which demonized her personally in a unique and
sophomorically sinister way. Delegates wearing buttons that satirized her circulated a book entitled *Hillar-
ious: The Wacky Wit, Wisdom & Wonderment of Hillary
Rodham Clinton*, a thin volume by right-wing writer
George Grant that parodied the rather innocuous fine
points of her many speeches and writings in the course
of a more general diatribe against gays, secular human-
ism, and the abortion-rights movement. The book be-

gins with an "Apologia" from the Book of Psalms, which reliably sums up its tone: "He who sits in the heavens shall laugh/He shall hold them in derision. Then He/shall speak to them in His wrath, and/distress them in His deep displeasure."

Some delegates to the convention objected to the book, saying it was not negative enough. They were out for the kill. And on the Sunday of the convention week a small faction, the Committee for Decent Family Values, obliged them. They held a "Rally to Stomp Out Hillary Clinton" outside the Astrodome, in the course of which a live elephant stomped on a doll that, so the group said, represented Hillary's "anti-family values." It was a strange bit of work for the Sabbath.

The most interesting of all the attacks on Hillary Clinton was made by a woman who, four years earlier, had herself been an object of ridicule in the press: Marilyn Quayle. Her pride still smarting from the fact that Bush aides had tried to "muzzle" her in 1988, and still angry about remarks that unflatteringly compared her hair style to Mary Tyler Moore's seventies 'do, she was like a bear with a burr in its side, scratching around in her wound and increasing her rage. The same woman who, just four years earlier, had said about the vice presidential ladyship, "Man, it's going to be tea and crumpets, and I would just go nuts," was now setting herself up as Hillary Clinton's polar opposite, a woman of the same turbulent generation who had happily chosen the path of tradition. Directing her speech to the baby boomers who did not "join the counterculture" or demonstrate or take drugs or "dodge the draft," she said, "Not everyone believed that the family was so oppressive that women could only thrive apart from it." Marilyn Quayle was at the time working as her husband's campaign manager, had a six-room office suite near his in the old Executive

Office Building, outspokenly corrected him in interviews, and left home to travel around the country on her book tour for *Embrace the Serpent*, a thriller she co-authored with her sister. Yet she bashed feminists: "I sometimes think that the liberals are always so angry because they believe the grandiose promises of the liberation movements. They're disappointed because most women do not wish to be liberated from their essential natures as women." She harped on the fact that the Clintons attend separate churches, forgetting the fact that in 1988, when stories had surfaced that her parents were followers of the fundamentalist preacher "Colonel" Robert B. Thime, Jr., known for his vicious attacks on homosexuals, liberals, and the United Nations, she had protested that religion was a private matter.

But in her own way, by taking center stage so forcefully and reclaiming the prominence denied her in 1988, Marilyn Quayle seemed to be trying to "out-Hillary" Hillary. The effort, though, ended poorly. When the Quayle crew screened their version of the biographical film shown at the Democratic convention, in which Hillary recounts how she met Bill Clinton in the library at Yale, Marilyn was seen delighting in telling how she met J. Danforth Quayle in a class at their law school: "We met over the death penalty." It just didn't have the same lovable vibe. Then again, as an insider told *Time* magazine, "Marilyn doesn't have a lovable side."

Barbara Bush, however, remained lovable, and even admirable, as she was caught by the TV cameras scowling and muttering to a companion during Buchanan's speech. She was moved to protest that the attacks on Hillary Clinton were "not my kind of campaign," and told the *Washington Times* that having reporters check out Hillary Clinton's personal life was "disgusting."

She later, however, gave a tacit nod of approval to the attacks on Hillary, saying they were legitimate "if it's a self-proclaimed co-president."

At the height of the anti-Hillary attacks at the Republican convention, Bill Clinton was led to wonder aloud whether "George Bush was running for first lady." He was not, but he *was* running Barbara against Hillary. That seemed an easier battle to win than his own against his Democratic challenger. Barbara Bush was twice as popular as he, and a significant portion of the population, throughout the campaign, had very mixed feelings about Hillary.

The Republican strategy, however, quickly backfired.

By Saturday, August 22, Bush campaign officials were privately asking convention speakers to soften their attacks on Hillary Clinton. Christian broadcaster Pat Robertson dropped all references to her in his speech. Mary Matalin seemed a prime candidate for the muzzle.

The Republicans had made a fatal miscalculation. The attacks on Hillary Clinton were supposed to resonate particularly well with older white southerners and northern blue-collar ethnic groups, both of whom were presumed to be suspicious of well-paid, independent women lawyers. But no one likes to see their mothers, wives, or daughters insulted. In criticizing working women, working mothers in particular, the Republicans had risked alienating the approximately sixty percent of married women who work in this country, not to mention the even higher percentages of unmarried female voters who do. They had insulted the way of life of the vast majority of American couples under age fifty. And they had further angered their constituent base among Republican women, many of whom were already considering defecting in response to the party's anti-abortion plank.

Jane O'Reilly, writing in the "Getting It Gazette," a feminist newsletter that was distributed at both conventions, summed up the feelings of many women when she said: "We are the political targets that Communism and runaway spending used to be. Women are now the enemy. Hillary Clinton is being presented as the 'other.' . . . But we are Hillary Clinton."

Of course, the real target of the convention attack was not Hillary Clinton at all. She was merely a symbol for the force that had wrought a sea change in the American family since the late 1960s, and had rendered it unrecognizable to those whose vision of domestic bliss had been formed along the lines of 1950s television sitcoms. Never mind that the social changes of the past twenty years had occurred across party, regional, and class lines and not, as the *American Spectator* asserted, simply among East Coast-educated, "affluent feminists." Never mind that the change had, to a large extent, been economic. The Republicans singled out Hillary Rodham Clinton, Bill Clinton's wife and partner, as the face of familial destruction. They said it was because she called for the destruction of the American family in her writings. Nothing could have been more untrue.

In building their case against the "family values" of Hillary Clinton, the Republicans relied upon out-of-context quotations and distortions of legal articles she had written as a lawyer and children's-rights advocate in the 1970s. Her most often quoted comment, the one trumpeted most blatantly by Pat Buchanan in his opening-night convention speech, came from an article she wrote in the *Harvard Educational Review* in 1973 entitled "Children Under the Law." In it she wrote: "The basic rationale for depriving people of rights in a depen-

dency relationship is that certain individuals are incapable or undeserving of the right to take care of themselves and consequently need social institutions
specifically designed to safeguard their position. . . . It
is presumed that under the circumstances society is
doing what is best for the individuals. Along with the
family, past and present examples of such arrangements included marriage, slavery and the Indian reservation system."

Although this statement was interpreted by conservatives to have, as Daniel Wattenberg of the *American
Spectator* put it, "likened the American family to slavery," it clearly did no such thing. It described how the
law had historically treated certain classes of people as
dependents on others, without the legal right to speak
for themselves. And in doing so, it simply reiterated
certain well-known facts. Until modern times, married
women had few legal rights and were considered legally dependent upon their husbands. Considered one
body under the law with their husbands, in the nine-
teenth century, married women in some states were
forbidden to own property in their own names or to
file lawsuits.

The fact that there were indeed clear parallels between slavery and marriage in the past in terms of the
distribution and administration of power was not a
radical concept. Neither was the thrust of the article. It
considered what the proper role of the state might be
in intervening in family life when parents were shown
to be incapable of adequately caring for their children.
It focused particularly on the issue of the need for children to have their own views expressed through court-
appointed representation.

Children had virtually no legal rights when Hillary,
as a lawyer for the Children's Defense Fund, wrote her
1973 article. Whereas delinquent children were pro-

vided counsel in court, the "dependency relationship" that children necessarily had with their parents assumed that non-delinquents did not have a separate right to independent legal counsel. This, Hillary Rodham argued, was a gross oversight, and deprived children of a fair chance to have their special needs and interests recognized by the law.

She suggested abolishing the legal status of minority, along with the presumption that children are legally incompetent, and said that all procedural rights guaranteed to adults under the Constitution should be granted to children whenever the state or a third party moves against them. In later writings as well, she made the point that the legal reasoning that characterizes as "minor" everyone under eighteen or twenty-one was artificial and simplistic and did not take into account the dramatic differences in competency among children of different ages. Hillary argued in favor of creating a scale of graduated maturity, through which the increasing competence of children would be taken into account.

Another frequently quoted statement of Hillary Rodham's comes from a chapter in a 1979 book *Children's Rights: Contemporary Perspectives*: "Decisions about motherhood and abortion, schooling, cosmetic surgery, treatment of venereal disease, or employment and others where the decision or lack of one will significantly affect the child's future should not be made unilaterally by parents." This was taken by conservatives to mean that she favored teenagers suing their parents to have a nose job or liposuction. But in fact, says Howard Davidson, an attorney and chair of the U.S. Advisory Board on Child Abuse and Neglect, "there's nothing in her articles that addresses the issue of children suing their parents." The citation at issue was actually part of a longer paragraph that sought to limit the kinds of "extreme cases" in which courts might intrude in resolving conflicts between children's rights and their parents. The whole issue of court or government intervention into the private sphere of the home is one in which her views have been particularly distorted.

Conservatives have called Hillary Clinton a proponent of more government inteference in the home. In fact, time and again in her writings over the years, she has argued that less is best. Although it is true that her idea of granting children competency would have made it easier for the state to remove them from parental control in abuse situations, Hillary Rodham was actually one of the first legal scholars to warn against excessive government interference in family life through social service agencies. And, according to Davidson, she did so long before lawsuits against state child-welfare systems for violating the rights of both parents and children became commonplace.

"It is important to recognize the limited ability of the legal system to prescribe and enforce the quality of social arrangements," Hillary wrote in 1973. Most families, she argued, are much better equipped to take care of children than the government, she wrote, expressing a fear of "arbitrary and harmful state intervention." The state "has the responsibility to intervene in cases of severe emotional deprivation or psychological damage if it is likely that a child's development will be substantially harmed by his continued presence in the family." But, she said, "the state does not provide an adequate substitute parent in many of the cases where intrusion is resultant in the removal of a child from his home." The thrust of the argument is that state efforts should focus on preventing abuse, not removing children from their homes once it has occurred.

An interesting point in Hillary Rodham's legal writing, which embodies an early version of the responsibility-minded social welfare views that the Clintons, as moderate Democrats, now espouse, comes in her assertion that granting children rights also means demanding of them responsibilities, and thus establishing a relationship of dual responsibility between parent and child. This idea was incorporated into state law in Arkansas when the state passed a requirement that pupils stay in school in order to receive and retain driver's licenses. This emphasis on personal responsibility, which runs through all Hillary Clinton's advocacy work, places her squarely in the moderate camp of social reformers, just as her emphasis on individual responsibility in the maintenance of the family situates her right in the mainstream of American political thought.

"Her basic position, that discrimination against children requires justification and that courts should have the opportunity to take children's views into account, is more or less taken for granted among people who have thought about children's rights," Sanford J. Fox, a professor at Boston College Law School and chairman of an American Bar Association committee on children's rights, told the *New York Times* in August.

The Republican portrait of Hillary Clinton as a radical has also focused at length on her strong ties to well-known liberal organizations. Criticism has focused in part on her tenure, from 1978 to 1981, on the Legal Services Corporation board, which she chaired for two years. Conservatives deplore the agency, which funds legal-aid clinics for the poor. They have hotly criticized some controversial suits that some LSC affiliates filed during Hillary Rodham's tenure. One suit, filed in Connecticut, asked the government to pay for a sex-change operation. Another sought giving over two-thirds of the state of Maine to Indian tribes. Even some

Democrats have criticized the agency's more controversial cases. But the agency is highly decentralized, and it is unclear how much control the board had over which suits affiliates chose to file.

Working for the Children's Defense Fund, a nonpartisan lobby, which Hillary chaired from 1986 to February 1992, also put her at odds with conservative interests and, at times, even with her husband. In 1991, the organization advocated increasing tax revenues by $11.6 billion by eliminating the tax break for inherited capital gains and by another $13 billion by doubling taxes on tobacco and alcohol.

The CDF also played a key role in Congress's childcare debate of 1990. That year Hillary Clinton made a two-week trip to France on a study team of child-care professionals. They visited schools and spoke with ministry officials, officeholders, educators, and health professionals. She was impressed by that in France there is mandated paid parental leave for birth and adoption of a child, preventive health services are part of child-care programs, and there are better salaries, supervision, and security for preschool teachers.

"What we saw was a coordinated, comprehensive system, supported across the political spectrum, that links day care, early education and health care—and is accessible to virtually every child," she wrote in an op-ed piece published in the *New York Times* that year. "Much more significant, though, are the pervasive beliefs in France that children are a precious national resource for which society has collective responsibility, and that one goal of a child-care system is to help children develop and thrive."

Her conclusions put her directly at odds with Republican orthodoxy: "Throughout the 1980s, debate over child care in the U.S. always seemed to focus on 'family values,' " she wrote. "This assumes that parents alone can always determine and then provide . . . what's best for their children and, hence, society. . . . But this view has allowed our government and, to a much larger extent, business to ignore the needs of America's children and their parents." She called upon the American government to learn a lesson from France. George Bush went on to veto every family-leave bill proposed by Congress.

Some of the CDF's positions pitted Bill and Hillary Clinton against each other. When the CDF lobbied for an array of federal standards governing child care, Bill Clinton, then head of the National Governors' Association, opposed them and won.

They also parted company on the ABC child-care program, a proposal designed to encourage national standards, centralized service delivery, and credentialized care-givers. Hillary strongly supported the bill, which Bill opposed, and it was defeated in Congress in 1990. Bill Clinton's own Arkansas child-care bill, like his education reforms, includes elements of parental choice.

Perhaps the most public conflict between them came in March 1991, when the Children's Defense Fund, along with fifteen other health and consumer organizations, sent a letter to House speaker Thomas Foley asking him to not act on a request from the National Governors' Association to delay an implementation of new Medicaid benefits for two years. The CDF argued that expanded Medicaid mandates were needed to ensure that pregnant women and children got the health care they deserved. Bill Clinton, as the head of the association, had been at the forefront of the governors' request. As vice chairman of the NGA's Health Policy Task Force, he had repeatedly complained that new costs incurred by the states under Medicaid were taking money away from education and other vital state services. He argued that the country had to find a way to deal with health care that did not involve sticking the states with additional burdens. Hillary, as chairman of the CDF, lobbied directly against him.

Articulating their differences of opinion was a delicate matter. "Bill's position, which is a responsible position for a governor to take, is more of a budgetary position," Hillary told the Arkansas *Democrat*. "Our position is a policy position. In the long run, this country is going to have to resolve the differences between the two."

The differences between their political views indicate that she is generally more liberal on social issues than he, and he is more attentive both to the fiscal bottom line and to how an issue will impact his political image. They have both been supporters of parental notification for abortion, though he has long opposed Medicaid spending. He did not begin to use the word "pro-choice" in reference to himself until the summer of 1991.

However slightly more liberal Hillary may be than Bill Clinton, she is far from a radical. In the late sixties and early seventies, she avoided radicalism, and she certainly did not move to the left after that.

Friends say that though she is generally somewhat more liberal than Bill, the difference is incremental.

"I think she's more liberal than he is," Carolyn Ellis says. "But they're both very pragmatic, and pragmatism has no labels."

Pragmatism, in fact, seems to be the ultimate defining label for the political philosophy of Hillary Clinton.

Friends attribute this in some part to her years spent in politics. "I think her views have become less ideological and more informed by experience," says Richard Stearns, a friend of Bill's from his Oxford days. "When I first met her she tended to have a more ideological approach to issues and decisions than she does today. Her views are still decidedly liberal, but they are not as reflexively liberal as they were when she was much younger."

The root of her political pragmatism may well be her religion, which is arguably the most central element in Hillary Clinton's life, after her husband and daughter. Every Sunday, if they're in town, Hillary and Chelsea can be seen in their regular pew on the left-hand side near the minister in Little Rock's First Methodist Church, a brick turn-of-the-century structure with a simple interior offset by two glorious rose windows. As a downtown church, located between the governor's mansion and the Capitol, it draws a racially and socioeconomically mixed crowd.

Attending separate churches is a matter the Clintons worked long and hard to resolve. The Methodist Church—started in the eighteenth-century by John Wesley, a British social reformer for the poor who spent his later life evangelizing among them—still preaches his gospel of social justice and personal and social responsibility. Bill's Immanuel Baptist Church is a far cry away politically.

"Methodism stresses the balance between the attention to personal, spiritual faith and social expression of that faith," Don Jones says. "The concern is for the underprivileged and the children, for the reformation of the world. That clearly is a strong part of Methodism, and it's not characteristic of the Southern Baptist Church. That is, they're very preoccupied with personal salvation, conversion, and that sort of thing. And while the Methodists don't eschew that, they tend to emphasize the social-responsibility side. That's what Hillary likes."

An incident that occurred during the Gulf War illustrated the difference between Hillary's progressive

church and Bill's conservative one. After church, on
the Sunday that churches across the nation had conse-
crated as a day of reflection on the war, the Clintons
met up with an old friend for brunch.

"What did the pastor say at your church this morning?" Hillary asked the friend.

"He prayed that all men and women everywhere
would be safe and no life lost," the friend, who had
attended a Baptist church service, said.

"Mine too," said Hillary, a teasing smile playing
around her lips. "And yours, Bill?"

His had been a rather hawkish call for a swift and
valiant American victory. He smiled and didn't say
anything.

There came a point, when Chelsea was about ten,
that for the sake of family unity, Hillary gave being a
Baptist a try. She attended Bill's church and sent Chelsea to the Baptist Sunday school. But the experiment
was short-lived. Though it was important to her that
Chelsea freely choose her own church affiliation, and
that the choice be as meaningful as Hillary's own con-
firmation into Methodism had been, she was nonetheless relieved when Chelsea chose Methodism. Dorothy
Rodham was glad too. She had been accused of blas-
phemy by Chelsea, who was then attending a
Southern Baptist Sunday school, for saying, "Oh, my
God," when she had accidentally knocked a glass off
her kitchen counter. Some of the lay Sunday school
teachers at Bill's church were extremely conservative.
She didn't relish the idea of a fundamentalist Southern
Baptist grandchild.

Methodism was strongly ingrained in the Rodham
family. Hillary's great-grandparents had been part of
the Wesleyan evangelical sweep through England. She
had grown into her own faith as a teenager in Don
Jones's Youth Ministry, and then continued her study

in college, reading theology by Karl Barth and C. S. Lewis, and studying the Old and New Testaments in academic framework.

She was not, however, as active a churchgoer in young adulthood as she has become in the last decade. She dates her full attention to spiritual matters to about twelve years ago, when she had a picnic in the backyard of the governor's mansion with Vic Nixon, the minister who had married her and Bill. He gave her a copy of the new Book of Discipline, and they discussed it. Afterward, she has said, "I was really ready to focus on spiritual matters again."

She has taught adult Sunday school classes in her church, and at one point she lectured around Arkansas about "what it means to be a Methodist." She has also made an effort to continue studying the teachings of John Wesley and other theologians throughout her adult life, and has impressed her pastors with her knowledge.

"She is so curious and open, her mind is so active in its pursuit of knowledge," Don Jones says. "She is literally a lay theologian."

Bishop Dick Wilke of the Arkansas area of the United Methodist Church agrees: "She understands the church beliefs biblically and theologically about as well as anybody I know. She's a Methodist by intellectual conviction. She's also done a great deal of study in the social positions of the Methodist Church, and I think she feels she's been guided in that direction."

What the combination of faith and politics means ideologically for Hillary Clinton comes down once again to the principled pragmatism her friends tie to her essence.

Reinhold Niehbuhr, the theologian who most greatly influenced Jones, wrote that humankind's capacity for justice makes democracy possible, whereas our inclination to evil makes democracy necessary. This dialectical way of thinking, Jones says, lies at the root of Hillary's world vision.

"She's more pragmatic than she is liberal ideological," says Jones. "And I think that her pragmatism has something to do with her faith. She is a deeply spiritual person. And I also think that her social concerns, her sense of social responsibility, rests on a spiritual foundation. Even her feminism. I think it's her faith that keeps her from becoming overly ideological about anything. If you're a secular feminist, it's pretty easy for feminism to become the religion, to become the lens through which you view everything. I don't think that could ever happen to Hillary. That doesn't mean that she is less concerned with feminist issues. But I do think that the extremely important thing about her personality is she will affirm something, like being pro-choice, but she's able to stand back and entertain some criticism of that position. When Bill was once making a decision about whether to commute a sentence with a capital punishment for a serial killer and rapist, Hillary agonized over this, asking me what I thought. And I said, 'Well, I believe there is such a thing as punitive justice, that's part of the whole concept of justice. And I think some people have forfeited their right to life because of the heinous deed that they've committed. And she said, 'Well, I think I agree with you.' But she was struggling with the question of could she conscientiously as a Christian say that. There was a tad of uncertainty about that. And I attribute that to her faith," Jones says. "It almost makes her dialectical."

Being a liberal, dialectical pragmatist in Arkansas often means taking positions that, at least in their view, don't conform to conventional American liberalism at all. Hillary has said that she believes that a culture of poverty exists. Her arguments for improving state education in the mid-1980s were made in the moderate language of job creation. During a campaign speech in September 1992 she endorsed Bill Clinton's proposed workforce reforms, which would require all able-bodied welfare recipients to return to work after two years of receiving benefits.

In August 1992, while promoting a new Arkansas initiative that offered coupons to pregnant women who sought early preventive medical treatment, Hillary called for a national health-care system, but she also spoke out for tieing welfare benefits to participation in preventive health care. "I hope we'll by tieing the receipt of benefits from the government to fulfilling health-care requirements for one's own family," she said, "One would not receive, for example, welfare benefits without proof that one had immunized one's children." It was the personal responsibility argument once again.

Hillary's positions on the boards of Wal-Mart, TCBY, and Lafarge, from which she earned close to $200,000 in director's fees over 1986 to 1991, hardly make her a foe of industry. But those connections served her well when she tried to gain business support for programs like HIPPY. But it did not create much goodwill when it was reported in April that a Ohio subsidiary of the Lafarge Corp., from which Hillary Clinton was earning $31,000 a year in director fees, was burning hazardous waste to fuel cement plants. The Ohio company, Systech, had been hotly attacked by environmentalists, community activists, and government regulators for polluting the environment. Whether or not Hillary had made board decisions affecting Systech is unclear. At the time she said that Lafarge was taking steps to dispose of tens of millions of gallons of hazardous waste that would otherwise have been dumped in landfills.

But critics saw great inconsistencies coming from a self-avowed environmentalist. Nevertheless, unlike Bill Clinton, who has consistently been labeled "soft" on industry after his defiant first term, Hillary is generally viewed as someone who seeks to find ways to put industry resources to socially enriching uses.

Hillary Clinton's active support of a drive to reduce the astronomical rate of teenage pregnancy in Arkansas was expressed in an odd combination of progressive and conservative terms. She advocated the project Adolescent Pregnancy Child Watch in the summer of 1986, saying it was essential to raise the educational possibilities for girls and young women. But rather than urging safety and contraception, she supported abstinence. "It's not birth control but self-control. It's all right to say no." It is morally wrong, she declared, "for children to engage in sexual activity. It violates every traditional moral code, and it unleashes emotions and feelings and experiences that children are not equipped to deal with." In her speeches, she issued a warning to young people that early pregnancy would ruin their lives. "They're valuable people. They should postpone sexual activity. They should get their education and think about the future."

On a more progressive, feminist note that same year, she made a statement calling for more certified midwives to fight rising rates of infant mortality, and expressed support for a midwife-training program at the University of Arkansas School for Medical Sciences.

Hillary Clinton's relation to feminism offers an interesting explanation of the language of her liberalism. Although she helped compile the state's "Handbook on Legal Rights for Arkansas Women" in 1977 and helped update it in 1980 and 1987, chaired the American Bar Association's first Commission on the Status of Women in the Profession, and has served on countless other panels addressing women's concerns in Arkansas and the nation, she is clearly wary of labeling herself a feminist.

"Most people don't want to be associated with some of the more extremist views that parade under that title," she told *U.S. News and World Report*. Though she sees the world through a feminist lens, she prefers to label women's issues as "human issues." She did this even when issuing her ABA report on the status of *women*, which found discrimination against women in law schools, job interviews, firms, and courtrooms, and concluded that there is a presumption of incompetence for women entering the field.

Some of this ambivalence about the use of the word feminist has to do with political viability. "She's always understood that if people aren't going to hear what you say, then you're not going to get your case made," explains Betsey Wright. "She doesn't in Arkansas go out and say I'm a feminist because that's one of those things that keeps people from hearing the substance of what you're saying. But she's not at all uncomfortable about it. She does recognize herself as a feminist, and to her that means an entire improvement of the status of everybody. She really believes that true feminism is letting every single person be free to be who they want to be and the best they can be. And she and Bill really share a lot of that."

Hillary Clinton has been known, however, to play the politician to a fault. When asked by *U.S. News and World Report* whether *Roe* v. *Wade*, the legal decision that granted American women the constitutional right to abortion, was a well-reasoned legal decision, she answered, à la Clarence Thomas, "I haven't thought about that in a very long time."

"She thinks women deserve equal opportunities, equal pay for equal work, and that women, just because they have ovaries, shouldn't shrink away from the challenges in life," concludes her friend Nancy Snyderman, also a feminist. "She genuinely believes that women deserve to be on an equal footing with men."

In a sense, whether or not Hillary Clinton calls herself a feminist is a moot point. Her life so embodies both feminist principles and feminist problems that separating theory from practice is meaningless. Hillary's sometimes seemingly uncharacteristic statements may simply be the latest outgrowth of her talent, so pronounced at Wellesley and Yale, for shuttling between discordant groups, communicating with all. Nowhere is that talent more in evidence now than in the way she talks about feminism. It is a dirty word to a great number of Americans, she knows, not least of all to Arkansans. And yet she has a great ability, most of the time, to pack a strikingly feminist punch into an often non-feminist delivery. This may in part explain why, in Arkansas, she has a devoted following among widely varying groups of women.

At a 1986 conference sponsored by the Arkansas Division of Aging and Adult Services, for example, her stand on women's issues was strikingly moderate. She said she knew it was "frightening" for women whose traditional social roles had changed so dramatically. She said as well that she wanted women to keep their traditional roles as the glue of families, but added that people had to recognize their needs for self-fulfillment. "I'm very concerned about women getting the worst of both worlds."

Speaking in July 1992 to young women in a classroom full of gifted high school students, she noted that the girls were loath to raise their hands, and said that she could empathize. Referring to the mixed signals that so often make even highly articulate, otherwise self-assured young women afraid to come forward, she said, "That's the kind of double bind that women find themselves in. On the one hand, yes, be smart, stand up for yourself. . . . On the other hand, don't offend anybody, don't step on toes, or you'll become somebody that nobody likes because you're too assertive."

She clearly knows.

Of all the charges leveled at Hillary Clinton by the Republicans, the charge of strident radical feminism is among the most ridiculous. Her life bears witness to years of traditional female sacrifice—if in untraditional ways. "If Hillary were doing what she most wanted to do in this world, she would not be a partner in a corporate law firm," her close friend and former Wellesley dorm mate Jan Piercey told Gail Sheehy. "That's what she's had to do—she's responsible for the revenue in the family."

She gave up her name to stand by her man. She deferred the dreams of her youth to follow his.

"*Personally,*" she told *Vanity Fair*, "I believe that a woman should put her family and her relationships—which are really at the root of who you are and how you relate to the world—at the top of your priority list. But I don't believe that I, or Barbara Bush, should tell all women that's what *they* have to put first. . . . What we have to get away from is the idea that there's only one right choice."

Choice is the cornerstone of Hillary's moderate feminism. She understands the barriers women face in making free choices, and sympathizes: "My friends who are full-time in the work world often regret not having a family," she said on the *Today* show in April 1992. "My friends who are full-time at home get that tinge of anger when somebody says, 'Well, what do you do?' And then many of us who are trying at different stages of our lives to balance both roles are afflicted by guilt and insecurity about all the things we're trying to do."

The having-it-all concept as we know it, she knows, is a sham. "We don't respect full-time housekeepers," she said. "We don't give the kind of income support families need so that more women could make that choice if they chose to do so. We don't respect the sacrifices and difficulties of women in the work force. We don't have family leave like many of the countries we compete with. We just need to take a deep breath and say, 'Look, women are trying in many respects to hold down two full-time jobs, and we're not making it easy for them to do that and they need to have more support and respect for that."

Her own life's odyssey of choices and concessions fills her friends with admiration. "Back in the seventies we used to joke that we'd shot ourselves in the foot, because in saying it was okay to have a career and everything else we ended up taking on too much," Connie Fails says. "But Hillary has established that you can have a balance if you set guidelines and restraints on yourself, not letting anyone else control you but controlling yourself. She's a role model for that."

What is clear above all else is that Hillary Clinton wants to be free to choose to call herself whatever she likes. In July of 1992, she told about two thousand delegates to the National Federation of Business and Professional Women's Club's annual convention that she would fight any attempts to pigeonhole her exclusively as a careerist or wife and mother. "I am all of those things and I am more than the sum of the parts: I am me," she said. "I've refused as best as I can and will continue to refuse the kind of stereotyping that tries to strip from me or tries to strip from anyone your individual dignity and your identity, because what I want

. . . is a community where we celebrate one another and where we recognize the complexity of who we are."

Perhaps the most pressing issue of Hillary's life right now is protecting her daughter. Although moving Chelsea into the national spotlight has heightened the problem, her concern in that area is not new. Ironically, given all the talk of her being an enemy of parental authority, she has proved over the years to be a very protective, even old-fashioned mother.

"I feel strongly that children deserve to have some childhood and some innocence and time to accommodate to the world of adulthood," she told *People*.

Hillary has always carefully screened what movies Chelsea could see, where she could go, in what social situations she could interact. Early fights have been waged over pierced ears—Hillary doesn't have them, and neither does her mother. She allowed Chelsea to see her first R-rated movie just this summer (*Lethal Weapon 3*—"Bill dragged us," she says.) But she refused to let Chelsea join her friends in attending a dancing class for boys and girls when she was ten, saying she was too young for that kind of co-ed social activity. In addition, though, she objected to the fact that the group seemed racially exclusive.

"She's been quite protective," says Ellen Brantley, a chancery court judge and the mother of one of Chelsea's best friends. "She is raising Chelsea in a rather old-fashioned way. She and her friends are not just dropped off at the mall. You can tell by the way Chelsea dresses and looks that she is not encouraged to grow up before her time. You don't see her going around with lots of makeup and inappropriate kinds of clothes. She's allowed to be twelve. Anyone who characterizes her as overly permissive or not concerned about family values is just ridiculous."

Chelsea is, without a doubt, the most important person in Hillary's life, and she describes herself as a "fanatic" as a mother. She rarely misses one of Chelsea's softball games or ballet recitals. She does homework with Chelsea by fax on the road. She came home from the campaign trail every few days just to be with her. She has said, though, that the concept of "quality time" is meaningless. She values "routine time"— playing games like Pictionary, Scrabble, and Hungarian rummy with Bill and Chelsea, going to movies or on trips, reading, going on shopping sprees. Mid-campaign, Hillary and Chelsea made a weekend jaunt to Hawaii. Friends say that together they're just like friends.

In bringing up Chelsea, Hillary has taken steps to pass on her deepest values: education, racial inclusiveness, tolerance, integrity. When Chelsea was six and resisted having to make her bed, the Clintons sat her down and gave her a talking-to, explaining that little girls didn't have maids picking up for them and that she'd have to learn to do things for herself. The Clintons have always sent Chelsea to public schools. She applied for the science magnet school that she currently attends through the lottery system, just like all the other children in her area. She is encouraged to pursue her interests with unflagging enthusiasm from her parents. "We have really worked hard to try to give her a sense of herself and be respectful of her interests and not try to mold her into some sort of little public image," Hillary told Charles Allen.

Chelsea, an eighth-grader who studies German, takes advanced math courses, and has inherited her father's fiercely competitive streak in playing games, seems unlikely to be amenable to molding. She is a bright girl who has skipped one grade already. She plays volleyball for her school and softball for a dentist-sponsored team called the Molar Rollers. But she likes ballet best, and has danced in *Nutcracker* productions in Little Rock.

The one insecurity Hillary has ever expressed has concerned her ability to provide a happy, normal childhood for Chelsea. It seems an odd fear for a woman who has made a specialty of looking after children's best interests. On the other hand, given her level of commitment, and her understanding of the pitfalls of childhood and adolescence in our age, it is perhaps all too understandable.

"Highest of all her concerns is trying to provide the absolute best family background for Chelsea, and there are times she has felt that it's very tough, that it's hard to grow up in that much of a spotlight, with two parents who have such significant, very public careers," her friend Eleanor Acheson says. "Hillary recognizes that parenting is tough under any circumstances, but in these extreme circumstances you have to work very hard. She's thought about it and worried about it and has done what she tends to do, which is to take it on and work extremely hard at it."

Perhaps the hardest work of all was weathering the Gennifer Flowers fiasco. How Hillary and Chelsea felt passing supermarket checkout lines adorned with Flowers's *Star* cover is hard to imagine. But Chelsea insisted upon watching *60 Minutes* with her parents. Sitting close, they all got through it together.

"What did you think" Bill asked at the end.

"I think I'm glad that you're my parents," Chelsea answered.

Given the facts of who Hillary Clinton is and what she believes in, the intensity of the reactions to her, from both right and left, is all the more puzzling.

"I really don't know what to make of it," Hillary told

Time. "I find it hard to take a lot of that personally, since the portrait is a distorted, inaccurate one. It's not really about me."

It is, perhaps, about everything but her.

Americans are just not sure of how they feel about the changes of the last twenty years. In that time the roles of men and women in marriage have shifted dramatically. Bill and Hillary Clinton reflect that change. They are a model for what the writer Naomi Wolf, author of the bestseller *The Beauty Myth*, has called the new "equal partnership family," or what Gloria Steinem has called "the family as democracy."

"The Clintons represent a kind of working partnership between husband and wife that we had not seen modeled before," says Democratic party consultant Ann Lewis. "But the lives they live are really more like more Americans' than the life that George and Barbara Bush live. Theirs was an older model that no one can afford or chooses to adopt anymore. But politics often lags behind reality. It takes longer for the political system to adjust to some of these differences."

The Clintons truly are the model for American families in our age. But public perceptions and acceptance of change evolve more slowly, sometimes, than change itself. American society has transformed itself irreversibly, but its population still clings to images of the past, fearful of the unknown future.

"Hillary Clinton represents something at once extremely terrifying and extremely welcome, depending on which part of the 'American people' you happen to represent," says Naomi Wolf. "She is the embodiment of the feminist future: a woman who combines feminist values with worldly power, in the form of her own sterling professional credentials and with her influence on her husband. To working women and women struggling to combine family and professional identities, this is an inspiring role model and a vision of a union between gender idealism and real power; but to those anti-feminists who see, in the triumph of feminism, a doubling of competition in the workplace and a doubling of male responsibility at home, she represents a waking nightmare."

Both men and women are threatened by Hillary's role as a highly successful working mother and spouse, says Jean Baker Miller, a psychiatrist at the Stone Center at Wellesley College and an authority on sex roles.

"Many women these days are made to feel that whatever they're doing, they're not wholly measuring up," Miller says. "So it may be hard for women to feel thoroughly good about Hillary Clinton. It reflects how difficult it is for them to feel thoroughly good about themselves."

The public's reaction to her, Miller says, is a projection of all the anxiety, misgivings, and fears that Americans have about the changes they have seen in their own lives. "Hillary Clinton had laid on her all of the kinds of conflicting feelings people have about the fact that women have made tremendous strides and yet still have a long way to go. The whole question of sex roles goes so deep for everyone that it's very hard for people to accept change."

In an interview with journalist Ellen Goodman last year, Hillary agreed that Americans have not yet come to grips with what it means to be an independent, strong wife—not to mention a wife in the White House. "I thought I understood that before this race was underway," she said during the Democratic convention. "That's what I was living. I thought that with some stops and starts and changes along the way, trying to get it all straight, I was a very lucky person because I had a profession that I valued, a marriage that

I thought was a partnership in the best sense of the word and gave me a lot of personal satisfaction.

"I thought I understood how to walk through that mine field of defining myself and striking the balance between my own needs and family needs that we all struggle with all the time. . . . I thought we [women] were beginning to develop a framework for that kind of life we could lead, still married, still committed to family, still engaged in the outside world. And I've just been surprised, I guess, by the assumptions that bear little resemblance to how all of us—not just me—make our way through this unchartered terrain. . . . We're all trying to work this out. We're all trying to find our way, and we don't have a common language. . . .

"I may be on the front line."

Clearly, the attacks at the Republican convention, extreme as they were, did not occur in a vacuum. Last year, according to a *Time*/CNN news poll, fully one-fourth of all voters said that their presidential choices would be affected by their views of Hillary Clinton. Of that group, almost twice as many voters said they would vote against Clinton as for him, based upon their dislike of her. That's a sizable number of people, and those are very strong views to hold about a candidate's wife.

But Hillary Clinton was more than a candidate's wife. She was alternately a demon and an ideal. As a demon, she proved that the old archetype of the scheming, deadly woman, invoked by the image of Lady Macbeth and described as a combination of "consuming ambition, inflexibility of purpose, domination of a pliable husband, and an unsettling lack of tender human feeling," as the *American Spectator* put it, dies hard in our society.

Historically, the angriest backlashes against powerful women have come at times when women in general were making advances in gaining political or economic power. The anticipation last year of great increases in the numbers of women brought into the U.S. House and Senate may have set off subliminal warning lights to many who—consciously or not—fear female power. As Brownie Ledbetter, who as a member of the National Women's Political Caucus in Arkansas has watched attitudes toward political women and Hillary Clinton change for more than a decade, puts it: "The Republicans just took the Year of the Woman and skewered us with it."

Hillary Clinton was just one of the casualties.

"Life can have some transcendent meaning," Hillary Rodham Clinton said to the graduating class of 1992 in an address following her acceptance of an honorary degree from Hendrix College, a Methodist College in Conway, Arkansas.

"Make a pact not to give in to selfishness or cynicism or hate. Cling to the enduring values you have been exposed to. Cling especially to the value that is given to all people and that is premised on their equal worth. Respect and trust individuals of all races, creeds, and colors. Work toward the achievement of a universal human dignity, not just your own personal security."

It was one of the most stirring speeches she's ever given. It might just as well have been a personal prayer. Delivered as it was in the heart of the campaign year, uttered, as it were, between the bullets of press and public attack, it was like a statement of faith.

Such statements, such faith, are what carried Hillary Clinton through the 1992 campaign year. She kept such thoughts close to her heart as she crossed the country, following the Clinton drama. A small address book filled with quotes from Scripture, poetry, and inspirational writings traveled everywhere with her. A

profound faith in herself and the worth of her beliefs
traveled too.

Hillary Clinton was mystified and hurt by the level
of vindictiveness in the attacks against her last year.
Yet even in the worst of times, the most personally trying, most insulting times, she reacted with a striking
degree of equanimity. She made it through the Republican convention without a single outburst of public re-
buttal or outrage. She was polite, even understanding.
It was almost as though she made an attempt to turn
the other cheek and forgive those who clearly knew
not what they did.

In defense of critics like Marilyn Quayle who attacked her, she told *People*, "So many of the baby
boomers suffered so many disappointments, at least
by their own estimation, in part because of the extraordinary competition for available jobs, available mates,
available everything. And because of that level of dis-
appointment, they really don't know what to think
about themselves, let alone somebody of their own
generation."

"We're all trying to make sense of how we live and
who we are," she told *U.S. News and World Report*.

Friends say that Hillary's equanimity is the most
unique, sometimes awe-inspiring aspect of her character. She has an incredible inner strength, an unusually
strong spirituality. This strength, they say, explains
why, despite her pain, her spirit was not broken by the
beating she took in the campaign this past year.

"It did not shake her or the core of her," her friend
Carolyn Ellis says. "Hillary has a beautiful capacity to
see the best in people. She can explain things to her
satisfaction, and then she doesn't react angrily."

When a number of campaign staffers advised that
she respond more aggressively to the changes leveled
at her by the Republicans, and perhaps start slinging

mud at Barbara and Marilyn, Hillary refused. *Let's wait and see*, she said. We know that what they're saying isn't true. The only thing we have to worry about is whether voters will think it matters. And I don't think that they will.

She was right. Faith won out over fear; vision shone through the political smokescreen. It was better to believe in the judgment of the people than to begin fighting fire with fire.

"People can overlook and ignore a whole lot of stuff that is thrown out into the atmosphere if they view it as irrelevant, tangential, or just downright stupid and nasty," she told *Newsweek*. "If you don't have a view of the world that is bigger than yourself, if the only reason that you're doing something is to fulfill your own personal ambition, then you can't sustain a campaign against that kind of concerted attack."

Hillary's refusal—aside from the Jennifer Fitzgerald slip—to fight back on the level of her rivals was about more than her ambitions in last year's campaign. It had to do with the ambitious task that she has set for herself as a person.

"I said to her back in April, 'You've hosted more teas than the rest of us will ever do in our lives. Why didn't you just come back and say this,' " Ellis says.

Hillary paused. She told her old friend, "That's not the way I want to be remembered at the end of my life."

8

Whither Hillary?

What kind of first lady will Hillary Clinton be?

The nation waits impatiently for an answer. All that is known so far is what Arkansas has seen. And Arkansans close to the Clintons say that what they've seen is what we will get.

"She'll be her husband's most loving support. She will be his best sounding board. She will be an adviser to him and his staff," says Betsey Wright. "And she will not push her way in. *She* will be sought out."

"She will be the best friend the children of America have ever had," says Little Rock educator Skip Rutherford. "And the White House will be more personable, more open, more inclusive, more fun than at any other time in America's history."

"She'll be what she's always been," says friend Carolyn Staley. "Bill Clinton's best friend."

Friend hardly covers the whole of it. As first lady Hillary Clinton will be, as she's long been, Bill Clinton's

most trusted adviser, his trouble-shooter, his ombuds-
man—some say, his conscience.

"She is strong where he is weak," reporter John Robert Starr says. "He may see the right thing to do, but
he will back off and look at the political consequence
of everything he does. Hillary, if she senses it's right,
will do it. She'll be his backbone."

In the weeks leading up to the inauguration, Hillary
wasn't saying much on the matter. The "Sphinx of Little Rock," as the *Washington Post* dubbed her, holed
herself up in her soon-to-be-former mansion home, refusing interviews, avoiding public appearances, and
letting the nation's curiosity simmer as she pondered
her role for the future. Friends and associates describe
a mood of reflection, a time of self-definition.

"She just wants to be so right in how she articulates
her position," Staley says, "because it's not just her
own, she's not necessarily speaking for herself anymore. She sees herself as being sort of a symbol for a
lot of American women, but wants to do it in a way
that's not confrontational, one that's easy, one that
hopefully commands respect and answers a lot of old
biases and misunderstandings."

Hillary, the perfectionist lawyer, won't say anything
if she can't say it right, and if she learned anything at
all on the campaign trail last year, it was to think long
and hard before she spoke, because there would be no
forgiveness for her mistakes. Once Hillary Clinton
starts thinking, avalanches of thought follow.

"She's a visionary," Nancy Snyderman says. "This
hasn't been a long run for a short slide. Hillary is re-
sisting being defined. People need to stand back and
let her be. She won't let the country down."

Soon the nation will know just what kind of vision
Hillary Clinton will bring to her first ladyship. She has

already made some things clear. She'll be a children's advocate, a voice for inclusiveness and diversity in the administration, for national health care, progress in the schools, possibly even for housing. She will speak for women, the poor and minorities. She will advocate better child and prenatal care and expanding Head Start. She will speak her mind. She will also try to bring a greater spiritual emphasis to the White House.

Without a doubt, whatever she chooses to do will go down in history, because Hillary Clinton will radically change America's notion of what a first lady can accomplish. She is strong, independent, unapologetically assertive, an equal partner both privately and professionally in her marriage. She is the first woman to arrive at the White House with a background equal to her husband's, an independent career as developed as his, and professional experience in policy activism on a par with his advisers. She is the first to have her own professional power base in Washington; the first whose only real disqualification from being a Cabinet member is the fact of being the president's wife.

"She will be a new type of woman in the White House," says Ruth B. Mandel, director of the Center for the American Woman and Politics at Rutgers University.

What Hillary's first ladyship will bring in terms of action is unclear. She will not serve in the Cabinet or any other high-level administration position. Barring that, however, anything is possible. Before the election, during the embattled month of August, she said that she was drawn to the idea of serving again on a special commission as she did in Arkansas nearly ten years ago, perhaps this time on a project to strengthen families. But by November, once the election had passed, Hillary quickly emerged as Bill Clinton's top adviser, with a hand in his major appointments and policy statements. At his first post-election news conference, he made Hillary's anti-tobacco views central to his defense of his appointment of Vernon Jordan to chair his transition board, when Jordan was questioned for being a board member of RJR Nabisco Inc., a tobacco-based conglomerate.

"Those of you who are familiar with my record and my wife's public statements here at home would have little to be concerned about us being too close to the tobacco lobby," Clinton said. The *Washington Times* headlined it: "LISTEN TO HIM, WATCH HER."

When Mickey Kantor was not selected as the next White House chief of staff, word was that Hillary had been one of the advisers who blocked him. She later sat at the table with her husband and his three other closest advisers deciding whom to choose for the Cabinet. She was seen as an important force behind Clinton's choice of Donna Shalala, chancellor of the University of Wisconsin, as secretary of Health and Human Services. Shalala, a liberal's liberal, is a friend and Children's Defense Fund colleague of Hillary's. Clinton's decision to focus his attorney-general search on women candidates was credited to her as well.

Bill Clinton has made no bones about Hillary's involvement in these matters.

"She advised me on these decisions," he was quoted in the *New York Times*, "as she has on every other decision I've made in the last twenty years."

Hillary also made news in November when she participated in Bill's first meeting with congressional Democrats.

"Stayed the whole time, talked a lot, knew more than we did about some things," Clinton said of her role after the meeting.

Top transition aides told the *New York Times* in December that they were often in more frequent contact with Hillary than with Bill. Some of them, obviously unhappy with the situation, said they were afraid of her.

Given all the influence that Hillary Clinton has wielded during a period of relative inactivity and isolation, the thought of what she will accomplish once Clinton is in office is awe-inspiring.

"She is involved now in all the decisions including policy discussions and Cabinet selection," a top official close to the Clintons says. "I don't think there is anything that is out of her reach as far as her involvement goes. I don't think there is anything, other than matters of national security, that she wouldn't be involved in."

Even before the election, Hillary put a great deal of thought into what being a first lady would mean. On the campaign trail she read books about famous first ladies and compared their experiences, looking for clues. But the lessons of the past were both enlightening and inadequate. Never before had there been a first lady of her professional standing. Never before had there been a first lady so uniquely a product of our age.

Not surprisingly, she felt her deepest affinity with Eleanor Roosevelt. While presenting Rosalynn Carter with the Eleanor Roosevelt Living World Award at a reception of the humanitarian group Peace Links, she noted that Roosevelt was energetically attacked by the press for speaking her mind well before Franklin entered the White House. "So the more times change, the less times change, apparently," she said. She vowed then that she would "make as much commotion as possible about issues that are important to the world."

Such comments have led to speculation that Hillary will follow the path blazed by the pioneering first lady of the Depression and war era, who visited the troops in the Pacific and in England, advanced the causes of African Americans and women, and traveled around the country serving as Franklin D. Roosevelt's "eyes and ears."

"She views Eleanor Roosevelt as an idealist, as somebody who made a difference," Kris Rogers says. "And I think that's what she's hoping to be able to do."

Like Hillary, Eleanor Roosevelt suffered onslaughts of criticism by the public and the press. Roosevelt's Interior secretary, Harold Ickes, told her once to "stick to her knitting." After her travels and advocacy for the poor angered both friends and foes of the president, anti-Roosevelt critics started wearing buttons saying, "I DON'T WANT ELEANOR, EITHER," and made a campaign issue of her liberal views.

But despite those similarities, Hillary Clinton is uniquely a first lady for our time. She has a professional training in politics and a power base among an influential group of male and female friends to further her work.

"Eleanor Roosevelt, for all her good intentions and her strong support system, didn't have anywhere near the professional training that Hillary Clinton does," says Betty Boyd Caroli, author of the book *First Ladies*. Hillary's training and stature will make an enormous difference in the way she is perceived in Washington and how she will interact with other professionals in the administration.

"I think that's one reason so many people are scared of Hillary Clinton," Caroli says. "She's really quite qualified to do anything she wants to."

Despite her independent activities, Eleanor Roosevelt was a much less threatening figure to traditionalist Americans than is Hillary Clinton. She was seen as an exception to her time, as an odd, quirky woman, and not as a standard bearer of social change.

"She was not seen as someone who threatened the male establishment or the political establishment," says Edith Mayo, curator of the exhibition "First Ladies: Political Role and Public Image" at the Smithsonian. "Now you have not only Hillary's activism and her intelligence and confidence in that field, but you also have her as a representative of a whole order of change in women's roles in American society and life. Now that the role of women has changed dramatically and women are doing more and more activism in public life, Hillary represents more of a threat."

Eleanor and Franklin Roosevelt's relationship could not have been more different from the Clintons. Not only were they personally estranged during their White House years, they also differed deeply on significant issues like civil rights.

As Franklin's emissary and information gatherer, Eleanor played a relaying role, but she was not invited to contribute to policy decisions.

"Mrs. Roosevelt had very little input on exactly what policy was going to be," says Lewis Gould, a professor of history at the University of Texas who teaches a special course on first ladies. "She could make a case to her husband, but more often than not, when the real decisions were made she'd be out on the road somewhere as his eyes and ears."

Franklin Roosevelt actually made a point of distancing himself from Eleanor's views on such issues as women's rights and racism. He disassociated himself from her on unpopular issues and basked in her glory when the public approved.

Neither Bill nor Hillary Clinton will be able to disavow anything said or done by the other. They have no such distance between them. She tests out his ideas, punches holes in his theories, comments on his speeches, and identifies the weak spots in policy. Neither of them will be able to disavow anything said or done by the other in the political arena.

"They have a partnership of many dimensions," Wright says. "It's more than parenting and the loving and the support system. There's a great intellectual partnership as well."

In such a partnership, the potential is much greater for shared power, and also for a blurring of the lines of who's involved in decision-making. That kind of potential for unauthorized decision-making by the person holding the first ladyship, "the only federal office from which the holder can neither be fired nor impeached," as the *New York Times'* William Safire has put it, is a sore point with the American public.

But, as *New York Times* columnist, Anna Quindlen pointed out last year, the public didn't elect James Baker, either.

Qualms about the personal, professional, and intellectual power of first ladies are not new. Such attacks are as old as the institution of the first ladyship itself.

Betty Ford was attacked for her advocacy for the Equal Rights Amendment, for which she actively lobbied legislators. Rosalynn Carter, who had represented her husband on diplomatic trips to Latin America, was so severely criticized that she could no longer be sent as his personal emissary. Nancy Reagan was criticized the most about her influence in political appointments or the firing of political operatives either inside or outside the White House. "It is a modern version of a theme that has run all the way through the history of first ladies, from Abigail Adams on to the present," Edith Mayo says. "And that is that any woman who is politically astute or who speaks her mind politically or who uses her position and influence is resented and ridiculed."

Like Hillary, the wife of William Jennings Bryan,

candidate for president in 1896, had a law degree. *Harper's Bazaar* labeled her an "intellectual" and ran her against Ida McKinley, the more traditional wife of the Republican candidate, who was labeled "feminine" and having "womanly qualities." In the debate over which woman would be better for the White House, Ida McKinley won.

Abigail Adams, wife of the second president, was called "Mrs. President" by critics who believed she wielded too much influence in recommending federal appointees.

Mary Todd Lincoln was said by her husband's opponents to be a southern sympathizer.

Edith Wilson, wife of Woodrow Wilson, who shielded her husband from public view after he suffered a stroke, reviewed all his documents and screened his visitors, until one senator complained, "We have [a] petticoat government!"

Hillary Clinton is not even the first president's wife to have expressed a disinclination for housework, evidenced in her "cookie" comment, and during her White House tour with Barbara Bush, when she showed a total disinterest in redecorating and wondered instead where she'd put extra bookshelves. She was merely following in the tradition of Sarah Polk, first lady in the 1840s. In Polk's campaign, when a critic said he was going to vote for James Polk's opponent because his wife made better butter, Sarah Polk answered that when she got to the White House she wouldn't make butter or keep house. She would advise her husband. That was quite scandalous.

What Hillary Clinton actually does as first lady may be less important than how she does it and how it's reported. Since first lady is largely a symbolic role, some observers assert that she may do whatever she likes as long as the symbolism is right.

"The power of this position comes from the press," says Sheila Rabb Weidenfeld, former White House press secretary to Betty Ford. "The first lady is a symbolic leader, and symbolism is so important when it comes to the press. You do something, and it has ramifications, whatever it is, whatever you say, whatever you do."

Rosalynn Carter was dubbed the "Steel Magnolia," and was blasted for sitting in on Cabinet meetings when in fact she sat in only once, in Walter Mondale's absence, and at Jimmy Carter's invitation. Those details, however, were not reported. As Mary Finch Hoyt, Rosalynn Carter's former press secretary recalls, it was not so much Rosalynn Carter's behavior as the portrayal of it that eventually gave the public the impression she had transgressed the boundary of acceptable symbolic behavior.

"Mrs. Carter started out with what the press said was a fuzzy image, and ended up with an image of being so powerful that she had to be muzzled by the White House staff," she says. "And she'd been doing the same things. She hadn't done anything any differently, any of the time she'd spent in the White House."

Symbolism can be changed; and painful though that may be it is necessary. Women have come too far to be held back for the sake of nostalgic beliefs. "I think it's time to change the role of a first lady and give her the freedom to be what she really needs to be for herself and her husband and her family," says Eleanor McGovern, wife of the former presidential candidate George McGovern. "Hillary Clinton is the new woman, and not all the country has kept pace with the idea of today's professional women. I think it's going to take some time getting used to, but I think it's good

for the country to have a first lady like that. Maybe it'll
help all the rest of us grow up a little bit."

It is always assumed that a first lady will have some
kind of power. What is often called into question is the
form that power takes. The relationship between first
lady and president has always embodied the nineteenth-century notion of public and private spheres,
whereby the male sphere in the morally compromising
realm of worldly affairs and the female sphere is the
morally incorruptible home. The arrangement, which
guaranteed the absolute exclusion of women from
public life, allowed Victorian men to feel that there was
always some moral realm preserved in their lives far
removed from the worldly sins of business. Most first
ladies have, at least publicly, made sure that their work
did not appear to break down this separation of
spheres. "Rosalynn Carter works in politics and government with Jimmy Carter, but she does it as a sub-
ordinate and his helpmate," Mandel says. "Barbara
Bush projected an image more of separate spheres, the
female: she did the children and the family, he did the
politics and government."

Dolly Madison served for a time as James Madison's
secretary, but she hid that from the public. Eleanor
Roosevelt could justify her activities by saying that she
was traveling for her husband, who was disabled, and
in that way was merely carrying out the traditional female role of care giver.

"Eleanor Roosevelt was always very modest saying
that she never gave Franklin advice, that she was
merely traveling and reporting back to him. She said
she was his eyes and ears doing what he couldn't do.
She was modest and would write letters to people saying: 'I don't want you to think that I influence Franklin
in any way.' " Caroli says.

Hillary Clinton will be the first to break down that

separation of spheres. Her power is worldly power, her tools are professionalism and experience. She will not even, like Nancy Reagan, who was otherwise considered a major power broker, have to work through the traditional, behind-the-scenes, quietly manipulative "feminine" route. She will simply participate. That directness, ostensibly a much more honorable route, may prove to be a problem.

"Hillary Clinton and her husband are pioneering in public an issue that I would say is as important as any other political issue, or more important than most, and that is an equal relationship between a man and a woman," says feminist author Gloria Steinem. "This will continue to be controversial because an equal relationship between a woman and a man is going against five thousand years or more of patriarchy."

Regardless of the political actions Hillary Clinton decides to take, she will bring a radical change to the White House simply by being who she is and in modeling the marriage that she lives.

"Hillary Clinton as an individual and the Clintons as a couple will have at least as great if not greater, an impact on the culture itself in the long run than whatever Bill Clinton does as president," says Mandel. "What they're going to be doing is defining new images and being role models for people as parents, as a married couple, as dual professionals. Bill Clinton is virtually unique, certainly at his level, as a strong man who is unthreatened by an equally strong and independent spouse. He is a man who will make it all right for other men to be more relaxed about liking women who are equally strong and independent."

By replacing Barbara Bush, who is loved but who represents the unreal past, with the model of herself and her family in the present, Hillary Clinton may lead the country away from imagining itself in ideal terms and embracing itself as it is. The simple facing of reality will be a radical change, and will affect the country more profoundly than any policy initiative or law could ever hope to.

"There are lots of couples like the Clintons," Mandel says. "But it's unprecedented for us to have a couple like that as highly visible and accessible as an image. By being who they are and doing what they do, Hillary and Bill Clinton will give people permission to think and act in ways already comfortable to them, but not heretofore publicly sanctioned by our dominant cultural images. They will give social sanction to styles of relationships that are already very common but haven't been played out in textbooks and movies and sitcoms and the places that set the tone and set the images for people to imitate. In them we have the first couple who will really give us permission to be who we already are."

Once the partisan politicking of the campaign year was over, the demonization of Hillary Clinton seemed to have miraculously vanished. All of a sudden, it seems, she was being canonized. She has become such a heroine to women that in late November, the *San Francisco Chronicle* commented that enthusiasts had elevated her to a status "somewhere between Wonder Woman and Cinderella." The *Washington Post* suggested that a "Hillary Cult" might be in the making. *Nightline* devoted a program to the issue. Even the Little Rock Airport Commission briefly considered rechristening the state's major airport, Adams Field, in her name.

Even the rumors circulating about her seem downright benevolent, WUSA-TV in Washington recently reported that Hillary Clinton wanted to be known as a "presidential partner"; she didn't. That she had gone back to using the last name of Rodham was denied too.

So was a story that she was gunning for the appointment of Anita Hill to a federal judgeship in Oklahoma.

The Presidential mythologizers are moving in fast.

Five months ago, in some people's minds, Hillary Clinton was the devil. Now she is an avenging angel— voice of the formerly disempowered, hope of the nation's women. Watching her rise has been thrilling, moving, exciting. It is easy to share in the wish to make her somehow superman. But somewhere, it must be remembered, that behind that smile, behind that voice, behind that headband—it's back!—a real woman lies. A woman who has suffered and triumphed. A woman with a dream for our time.

What kind of first lady will Hillary Clinton be? Who will the American people allow her to be? We forget the truly important question: Who does she want to be?

Perhaps the greatest aspect of the power that Hillary Clinton is about to receive is her ability now to be who she wants to be. By doing that, she will be the best model for women, girls and families in the nation. "Like children, we don't do what we're told, we do what we see," Gloria Steinem says. "And so to set the example here will be very important."

The right to choose—Hillary Clinton will model it in the choices she makes this coming year. The right to be herself—it worked in Arkansas; it can work again here.

"Hillary Clinton has an opportunity to create an identity for herself, and if she's convinced that it's what she wants then the American people will accept that," says historian and biographer Doris Kearns Goodwin. "The American people's attitudes towards what they want are so ambivalent, and confused, and uncertain that, if she's confident about it, she can make the country respond to her definition. And that is the important lesson of Eleanor Roosevelt, that by the end of her tenure, people accepted who she was. The lesson from the campaign is that Hillary needs to define herself for herself and not carry anymore about what others are going to think. As long as she is comfortable, then I think the country will respond."

If the country can come to see Hillary, a woman so demonized and loved, as a real person who happens to be in politics; if the country can adjust to the fact that she is who we are and not who we never were but would like to be; then a great step forward will be made in our country's ability to see women as full people, as actors and not just as receptacles for our hopes, fears and dreams. If Hillary Clinton can help change that, then a whole new world will open up for women with political aspirations. She herself may have passed up her chance at political office in Arkansas; she may have passed up the path to attorney general or Supreme Court justice; she may not have put herself in the running to build a power base and run for president, but one thing's for sure, by being in the White House, modeling power, professionalism and partnership, she will pave the way for other women in the political generations to come.

And who knows? Maybe the economy, this awful mess, will do Bill Clinton in after all. Maybe the election in four years' time will be yet another grueling fight for the Comeback Kids. Maybe, as the Quayle-Buchanan ticket heats up for '96, Clinton, spouse alongside, will take them on, punch for rhetoric punch barefisted. Maybe Clinton will make history.

Hillary, that is.